JOURNEY *to*
Lessen the Gap
BETWEEN SCRIPTURE
and PSYCHOLOGY

SHARON PRIEST MSW RCC

AND KATHRYN COLEGRAVE

DISCLAIMER

This is not a self-help book, and for more information please research and find information on archetypes and abandonment. It is our intent to provide enough information to demonstrate that perhaps psychology and scripture can meet.

The contents of this book may call to mind memories of past traumatic events. If you are in need of support, call your nearest Crisis Line.

◆ FriesenPress

One Printers Way
Altona, MB R0G 0B0
Canada

www.friesenpress.com

ISBN
978-1-03-831261-7 (Hardcover)
978-1-03-831260-0 (Paperback)
978-1-03-831262-4 (eBook)

1. RELIGION, CHRISTIAN LIVING, PERSONAL GROWTH

Distributed to the trade by The Ingram Book Company

TABLE OF CONTENTS

ACKNOWLEDGEMENTS AND DEDICATIONS

Acknowledgements from
Sharon Priest

I AM ACKNOWLEDGING MY children who were on the journey with me as I healed. They were God's gift to me and kept me from travelling down many dead-end roads. They supported and encouraged me every step of the way as I struggled to overcome demons and put my journey on paper. Thank you. I think you are remarkable adults. I would also like to acknowledge my therapist Susan Breiddal for the countless hours she spent listening to me and accepting me. Gratitude to my foster family Keith and Susan Lingwall who taught me how to be in family. Many friends and supporters along the way are truly appreciated. Last and not least, thank you to my co-author Kathy Colegrave, who stuck with the process and was willing to struggle alongside me. Thank you for your commitment, support, and dedication.

Acknowledgements from
Kathy Colegrave

I WANT TO THANK and acknowledge my husband, Ray, who has always supported me in my decisions and work, making space for my projects and providing patience while I am on the journey. There are so many other people to thank, too many to list. Teachers and friends who nurtured my faith and healing, providing strength and encouragement along life's pathway. My children, my grandchildren, and friends who love me for who I am with all my faults and scars and wounds; you give me courage to break out of my comfort zone. Thank you for your love and patience. Most of all, I would like to acknowledge and thank my co-author, who initiated and is the driving force behind this book. Thank you for including me on the journey.

Sharon's Preface
(Part 1)

I THINK MOST PREFACES and introductions are short. Mine seem to be quite wordy. Both the preface and the introductions set the stage for meaning and understanding the concepts and ideas set out in the rest of the book, so I urge you to read them both.

This book is based on three concepts, scripture from the NIV Bible (1995), (unless another version is specified) and two psychological theories, Archetypes and Abandonment. Our objective is to share enough that the reader, whether believer or nonbeliever, can explore the concept that psychology and scripture can meet and enhance healing. It is not a choice of either-or, which seems to be the way it is seen in today's view. We would like with this book to lessen the gap between scripture and psychology. To lessen the gap takes a conscious willingness to explore and to want to understand the self. Both psychology and scripture embrace the belief that to heal, to make sound decisions, one must examine their heart, which means examine their beliefs and values. To embark on this spiritual, emotional journey takes courage.

Well, this writing journey has turned into a saga. We began in 2018 and here we are in 2023. We have been in a lockdown state due to coronavirus since March 2020. The world is isolating. No visiting with other family that are not part of your household. Essential services only are working. Travel only for necessities. We are having most things delivered. Social distancing protocol is to remain six feet apart in stores, when walking, or during doctor visits—in all social situations. Healthcare, as much as is possible, is delivered online. Doctors are returning calls, diagnosing, and prescribing via phone. I like that service. Masks are to be worn and hands are to be sanitized in and out of venues.

My life has not changed a whole lot because I am essentially a hermit anyway. I miss the rest of my family and doing group work in the community I have worked in for the last six years. The world is grieving. There is loss on so many levels; thousands and thousands have died, all schools and children's activities are closed, and even spaces like parks can be restricted. We're experiencing a huge existential grieving. The energy level impacts everyone, and for some, it is very palpable. I think many people, sometimes myself included, react to the loss of choice about how to live our lives. We are mandated to follow medical protocols. Having choice taken away can be experienced as a loss of autonomy, and someone who has been interfered with in any way growing up may experience huge anger. This is an interesting time, for sure. I wonder in five to ten years what society will see as ramifications to the isolation, especially in those children who spent the first three years of their lives wearing masks and in some form of isolation.

Now that I have given some context to the time we are writing in, I will continue to provide specific background to the book. Some questions to assist me in doing this are: How come we are writing this book? How come at this time? How come I, Sharon, am writing with this co-author? What is it that we hope to accomplish /convey?

How Come This Book?

My hope is that I can, in some small way, communicate my belief through my experiences and knowledge that there can be a complementary coming together of psychology and scripture. Through sharing, we can provide an understanding of each concept in a manner that promotes healing from emotional wounds and delivers information allowing each reader to make an informed decision about which direction their healing path will take. It is my belief that at each crossroad we have an opportunity, a choice, to either draw nearer to God or turn away. We have a choice to take our healing journey or not. It is my belief that we all take our journey and answer at some point for our choices. Or perhaps this body of work will inspire someone to search out an alternative modality or theory to begin to address past wounds and embark on their journey. It is not my intent to judge anyone or set out a path that I think people "should" or "need to" follow.

How Come These Concepts?

I want to share these concepts because they spoke to me, and my hope is that they speak to others as well. The concepts of abandonment from the book *The Journey from Abandonment to Healing*, by Susan Anderson; the six archetypes, Innocent, Orphan, Altruist/Martyr, Wanderer, Warrior, and Magician, as defined by Carol Pearson in her book *The Hero Within*; and scripture from the New International Version (NIV) translation of the Bible seem to fit together in a way that makes sense to me and offers a more inclusive way of healing. I am reminded of verses here: "All Scripture is given by inspiration of God and is profitable for doctrine, for reproof, for correction, for instruction in righteousness" (2 Timothy 3:16). A second is from Matthew 22, which talks about how after washing the inside of the cup, then the whole cup will be clean, as well as not putting new wine in old wineskins but putting it in new wineskins. This speaks to me of beginning the journey of healing from the inside out.

How Come at This Time?

Well, I do not have an answer for that question exactly. I have stated for years I was going to write a book. People have asked if I would write a book comprised of some of the topics I teach in groups. All I can say is that I think all those times when I thought "Yes, I will write a book," I was working according to my timing. This time, it seems like it is God's timing. That may sound arrogant—you might be asking, "How do I know that?" Well, all I can do is walk through an open door in faith. I know by experience if I really push and struggle to "make" something happen, it is usually my own plan. When I act on plans or ideas that are seemingly of God's design, the way seems easy:

> For I know the plans I have for you. Plans to prosper you
> and not to harm you, plans to give you hope and a future.
> (Jeremiah 29:11–13)

I have been downsizing as I scale back my professional work, perhaps in preparation for some kind of retirement or shift or transition. Part of that downsizing included donating books. which to me is like cutting off my right arm. My children detested moving time because there were more boxes of books than other items. Originally, I was going to donate *The Hero Within*, and as I was going through the donation box one last time (just to make sure), I opened the book. I have read this book quite a few times, and I had an idea of what the book contained, so other than the fact that I am a bookaholic and I hurt to give a book away, I am not sure why I opened the book at all. The book opened to its pages on The Warrior archetype. Of course, from my own recent experiences of downsizing, moving, and the loss of my brother after looking after him for some time, I was seeing myself in a way I had not noticed before. About a half hour later, I was still reading and becoming excited because I was connecting Pearson's ideas to abandonment concepts from Susan Anderson's book, and then scripture was coming to mind, and the idea of writing about these three concepts was born. I had not felt that level of excitement in some time. Other than the idea, however, I had no clue how to move forward.

Why Am I Writing with his Co-Author?

I was meeting my friend Kathy for lunch with no intent of asking her to write with me. I really respect Kathy's honesty, insights, knowledge, and her willingness to grapple with issues. I see Kathy as a detail person, which is necessary for me to have in my life. This quality seems to give me a sense of balance, as I have the vision or the plan or idea, and once I execute that, I say, "Oh well I am done now; on to the next."

At lunch, Kathy was sharing that she had been praying and asking God to put something meaningful in her life that she would enjoy doing. We chatted on, and then I was sharing about my idea for this book. She listened in silence and then said she had goosebumps. I then asked if she would like to co-author. I was flabbergasted that those words came out of my mouth! That was a little over two or more years ago, and I am blessed beyond belief at the journey we have shared while grappling with the issues arising from within as we write. So much personal work at such a great depth was explored, shared, and healed to some degree before we could even begin to write. Reading brought up many issues, and as I explained Susan Anderson's work to Kathy, I was faced with deeper, unexplored layers of my family of origin wounds. (Family of origin refers to the people you grew up with; the people you live with in childhood.)

What a gift being in the space in between, the liminal space! A liminal space is the transition between where you have been and where you are going. This space can be scary and so exhilarating at the same time. Quite paradoxical. In this space, mental sets break away to allow for new mental sets to be created, a new, different way of making sense of myself, others, and the world. There is also at play the dynamic of joy and the beliefs surrounding this emotion. Growing up as I did where joy was taken away, ridiculed, or was a shaming experience, the message becomes very clear and then unconscious. The message is do not show or feel joy or happiness because "bad" things will happen.

Joy and pain become marriage partners. This belief is acted out unconsciously until we make it conscious and change the belief.

As I write, I realize that I have a belief that sabotages me from being successful. Reading and preparing to write has of course, unearthed many family of origin issues. Our beliefs are in place by about age five. My overarching, unconscious, sabotaging belief is that no one wants me, that I am not valued so therefore I have nothing of value to contribute, and that I will be rejected and alone always. One of the ways I act this out is through the action of being less than I am, or not being successful, because my past experience in my family was that if I was smart, or smarter than my younger brother, or if I pointed out parenting inconsistencies, then I was ridiculed, called names, treated as different than my siblings. Teachers would often become angry at me because I was not working to potential. I was not ever really encouraged, nor was I shown how to reach my potential. One year I made the honour roll in high school, and my dad called me stupid because I should have done that the year before! He gave my younger brother, one grade behind me, $20 just for passing. My father's action created a horrible feeling for both my brother and me. Succeeding or doing well seemed to bring attention to me in a very hurtful way. I so wanted someone to give me some caring encouragement and attention. I learned to not draw attention to being smart.

I never had my own room. I slept on the couch and had a drawer in my parents' dresser. I did my chores and my brothers' chores. I had to eat whatever was being served while my brothers could choose. In a discussion with Kathy, I was sharing these memories with her, and the next morning I realized the far-reaching impact these experiences have had. It is not the experiences themselves, however; **it is the meaning a small child makes of these types of situations and the beliefs that arise from repeated messages.** I have known this concept for most of my professional life; however, in the light of this work, I see the impact on my life in a very different way. I was very alone with these childhood experiences. I had no one to tell or to confide in, who would help me see things in a different way. I did not have anyone to comfort me or witness or advocate for me. When a group of girls in Grade 5, including myself, went to our most adored and trusted teacher to tell her and ask for her help because the principal was sexually molesting us, she closed the door in our faces, saying she couldn't help us. There goes my safe place, and a mistrust of women in authority was born, fueling an anger that was already smoldering. So, I have struggled in my teen and adult years and in my professional career when most not-for-profit organizations are comprised of and led by women. Being alone, not being connected or not having anyone to tell, is what contributes to creating trauma; it is not merely the traumatic event.

These childhood messages and the meaning I made of them have led to a huge pattern in my life, which will play out in the book in all three concepts, abandonment, archetypes, and scripture. I am very grateful to God for putting Kathy in my life in the role of friend and co-author sojourner to explore this book and this path of healing. Of course, I had to examine if this was just a repeat pattern of not being able to do something on my own because I did not want to shine too much. After prayer and a diligent soul search I concluded that no, I believe this book is a God-driven project. Whether we publish or the writing is only a vehicle to allow deeper healing for ourselves, it will serve His purpose, whatever that may be. Also, I believe God is in the timing and planning because this book fell into place without either Kathy or I having to prod and push.

Why These Topics?

I have listened to many sermons by many pastors in many different denominations. The overall message I have received about counsellors and psychology has not been flattering nor inspiring, to say the least. In fact, counselling has been denounced as against God; it's also been said that counsellors, unless they are Christian counsellors, will lead you astray and away from God (I am not sure what this statement may say about God). I do believe the statement to be untrue. I know Christian counsellors who struggle and judge their Christian clients in a very demeaning unchristian way, saying things like, "What's the matter with them? They are Christians. They are supposed to know better." I think this is an example of needing to remove the plank from your own eye first. Judge not lest ye be judged. Yes, we have a responsibility to hold each other accountable as Christians; however, we are to do so in an attitude of love and grace.

My belief is while it may be easier to speak with someone who speaks the same language or has the same beliefs, there are also many benefits to speaking to someone who does not share similar religious beliefs. I think a counsellor who is self-confident and has done and continues to do their own personal work can assist someone else to do likewise without projecting their beliefs onto their client. A counsellor's role is not to change the client into someone else. Their role is to assist the client in exploring their own beliefs, values, and behaviours, to explore how their lives manifest their beliefs or don't. My responsibility as a Christian is to ensure my actions reflect my Christian beliefs by meeting all with love, respect, grace, and acceptance as all have inherent worth. I know that in my work some people have explored and embraced Christianity because of the work they did in their counselling sessions. I am by no means saying that scripture is found in all psychological theories. However, I do believe it is found in many theories and it is our hope that these theories will assist in beginning their healing journeys.

Kathy's Preface
(Part 2)

There is a time for everything, and a season for every activity under the heavens: a time to be born and a time to die, a time to plant and a time to uproot, a time to kill and a time to heal, a time to tear down and a time to build, a time to weep and a time to laugh, a time to mourn and a time to dance, a time to scatter stones and a time to gather them, a time to embrace and a time to refrain from embracing, a time to search and a time to give up, a time to keep and a time to throw away, a time to tear and a time to mend, a time to be silent and a time to speak, a time to love and a time to hate, a time for war and a time for peace.

(Ecclesiastes 3:1–8)

The time is right to continue and finish this book. It has truly been a long-haul journey. In 2018, I wrote these words:

All things have a beginning and for me this is one of them. I'm not sure where I'm going or what will come of this, but I have thrown my hat into the ring and I'm about to start to write a portion of this book. It is exciting, scary, and seems beyond my capability sometimes, but the journey has begun for good or ill.

I wrote this before COVID changed our lives and our perspectives on life, before masks were commonplace, and doctor's appointments were virtual. Since then, I have been in and out of hospital twice, undergone major surgery, and experienced COVID myself. The antibiotics I needed caused changes to my eyesight, and I couldn't read for a time without extreme frustration and headaches. However, with healing and a new prescription for my glasses, I am back, and it's time to finish this book and close this chapter of my life. God is good!

In the following pages, I will endeavor to illustrate the overlaps and entwining roles of scripture and psychology through archetypes. I have faced the spiritual/psychological barrier on many different levels during my lifetime so far. Whatever life throws my way, I find solace, hope, and strength in the scriptures, but sometimes along the way, it seems I come to a crossroad, and I find myself floundering across the imaginary line drawn between the church and psychology. When I am at a loss as to how to continue my journey, I need to understand my reactions and how to best relate to others. Archetypes help me to understand me!

Dictionary.com (n.d.) defines an archetype this way: "(in Jungian psychology) a collectively inherited unconscious idea, pattern of thought, image, etc., universally present in individual psyches." My understanding from a psychological perspective is that we each act out our own stories that are defined and based on our assumptions of the world around us from both a conscious and an unconscious understanding. During the hero's quest, we journey to find our true, authentic self. To do so, we each commonly take on and circle through personality archetypes.

I'm not sure where the writing of and consequent finishing this book will take me. I knew even before I struck the keyboard with the first letter of the first word, I had learned much about myself. I continue working towards healing. Understanding that the more healing I do in my life will dictate how healthy my interactions are with others, particularly my family, has changed my entire outlook on life. Talking things through with Sharon to come to a clear and consistent understanding of our mutual goal, our mission in writing this book, has been illuminating. Sharing my experience in writing has been soul wrenching at times. I have realized that I have not shared this part of myself with those closest to me out of fear, but now, realizing it will be out there, as they say, a kind of freedom has swept over me. I am the person God created me to be and, therefore, I am good enough! Looking at my background, my childhood, my life through the archetypes is an amazing, wonderful, and freeing experience. My hope and prayer is that the same can be said for you, the reader. I know a change in perspective can change everything!

GENERAL INTRODUCTION

READING THROUGH THE writings, we decided we needed to give a brief general introduction and then individual ones. We come from different backgrounds of learning and knowledge. As a result, we see and understand from both a shared and different lens. Our writing styles are very different. Sharon writes from a teaching and workshop perspective. Her education and experience is in the field of social work and clinical counselling. Kathy writes with an academic style, educated in the field of Pastoral and Children's Ministry. Therefore, Kathy has written a brief Introduction and Sharon has written Setting the Stage, by way of introduction.

The book is not an in-depth exploration of abandonment or archetypes. Our hope is that we have shared enough to demonstrate the connection between scripture and psychology. We are not saying that scripture is found in all psychological theories; we are saying that some concepts share and teach the same tenets perhaps in different ways.

This writing is subjective, and interpretations and meanings are made from our personal observations, situations, and experiences. This is not written from an academic standpoint, and we will quote or give references when they are from a different source other than our own experiences and meanings.

KATHY'S INTRODUCTION

"He has made everything beautiful in its time. He has
also set eternity in the human heart; yet no one can
fathom what God has done from beginning to end."
Ecclesiastes 3:11

I UNDERSTAND MY TIME is not my own, but God's timing is everything. I am shaking my head and praising my wonderful, surpris-
ing, and loving God! I am at a crossroad, and I have been in a desert
place in my life's journey for a long time. I had set off on various paths,
but I knew I had not found the next chapter in my journey with God.
His answer to my prayers was to wait. Then one day, my friend Sharon
and I were having lunch together and she mentioned a book she was
rereading, *The Hero Within* by Carol Pearson. As she told me a little bit
about the book, I found myself intrigued and curious, but not excited,
to learn more about the psyche because in my experience that kind of
learning often involved change. Though I felt stuck, I was too tired
to change. However, the more I thought about it, the more drawn I
was to the ideas and concepts Sharon shared, and when she asked me
if I'd like to collaborate on a book exploring the archetypes we live by
while drawing in and interweaving Christianity and healing, sparkles
danced in my brain! This was the challenge, the path, the opportunity
that I long awaited!! Though terrified and constantly wondering why I

thought I had enough interesting thoughts and information to share, I responded to Sharon immediately—I'm in!

I have been married to my loving husband for thirty plus years. We have two adult children, a boy, and a girl. Both are married, and I have three beautiful granddaughters. I accepted my Lord and Saviour at seven years old, but it wasn't until many years later that I began to consistently walk with Him. That was many years ago, and during that time, my life has been a journey through good, bad, and even evil times. Over the years, I have looked at my life and wondered, where is God? If He loves me, how can this be happening? When will He show up and make things right? What I have learned is that He is the one constant in my life. He is always with me, and His love never fails, even when I can't see Him or when I am misbehaving. In hindsight, I can see His hand in every situation, and I am humbled and thankful for His healing power. I praise and thank Him for what he has done and continues to do for me!

I am ready for this next challenge, and I am both excited and fearful at the same time! I have always wanted to write a book, and often people have said I should write one, but I could not find a focus or the confidence to begin. Now God has given me another gift, another opportunity. Though I am afraid, I know nothing is impossible with God and He will never leave me, so here I am taking on this challenge with my co-author. writing a book where I will share my journey through the archetypes we live by, my healing from life's experience, and my understanding of God's never-changing, overreaching love, which touches every aspect and moment of my life. Even as I begin, I know my psyche will be stretched, and there will be times of frustration, yet there will also be joy on the journey as I work and wrestle with thoughts and concepts. My fervent prayer is that God will use the pages of this book to encourage, to inspire, and to strengthen. It will all be worthwhile if even one person benefits in some small way from the read. Prayerfully and sincerely, I give these pages to God and to you, the reader. "Now faith is the substance of things hoped for, the evidence of things not seen" (Hebrews 11:1).

Setting the Stage
and Introduction to
Abandonment (Sharon)

"Your word is a lamp to my feet and a light to my path."
—Psalms 199:105

I BELIEVE MOST PEOPLE do not read introductions. I urge you to read this, as the information contained here sets the stage for understanding the concepts of the two psychological theories that are used in the book. We have added personal stories to add clarity and understanding.

Format

Finding a format meant returning to the drawing board many times. Kathy and I struggled. We would think we had a format that would work, and we would begin to work with that idea, and then one of us would find the flaw or the gap that would not allow us to do what we wanted to do. At times I can say I was frustrated, and I also knew that a way would be made clear. We finally decided that the format would be the same for each chapter. We ended up with each chapter being titled by an archetype, followed by the stages of abandonment from

SWIRL. This is followed by how scriptural teachings can be found in both concepts. We end each chapter with our personal experiences of archetype, abandonment, and Christian life as informed by scripture.

SWIRL

SWIRL is the acronym Susan Anderson (2000) uses for the stages of abandonment grief. SWIRL stands for shattering, withdrawal, internalizing the rejection, rage, and lifting.

Ms. Anderson's concept of abandonment introduces us to the inner child or Little, the outer child or Chuckee as one group named it, and the adult or Big. Little is the small child about three years old who is very fearful of being rejected, abandoned, or experiencing any type of perceived loss. Little has the fear feelings.

Outer child or Chuckee as I will refer to this character is nine to eleven years old. Chuckee's job is to take Little's fear away and to keep all the patterns the same. Chuckee does this by fight, flight, freeze, faint, fawn or fornicate. Keeping Little attached at all costs is one of the goals.

The important piece to remember is Chuckee is only activated when Little has been frightened by a loss or a potential loss, and the adult has not regulated or soothed the feelings, which brings the adrenaline down. When Little is frightened, we usually take a "caught" breath, I call it the clutch, and tense up somewhere in our bodies. This sends a message to the brain that there is danger. The brain does not know the difference between a real threat or an imaginary one such an, "oh no! What if he/she is mad? What if I lose my job?" The brain, the amygdala, is then alerted to send out messages to get the adrenaline pumping to survive. It is the task of the Adult part of us to stay present, which would mean we are in the frontal cortex of our brain, and differentiate between real and imaginary threat, the present situation or a memory activated from a similar past situation.

The prefrontal cortex of the brain diminishes beginning in young teens and for males it does not come back in until about twenty-five years of age. So, cause and effect, impulse control, analytic processes are limited. Prefrontal cortex is referred to as the executive functioning part of our brain regulating our behaviour.

S—Shattering

Shattering is the first stage when the abandonment first happens; feelings experienced, according to Anderson, include shock, pain, and panic. Faith and trust are shattered, and there is a severing of the bond. You may feel you cannot live without your lost love, and these may even be suicidal feelings. Remember, feelings are ONLY TEMPORARY. FEELINGS DO NOT LAST!

Symptoms may include:
- Feeling helpless and dependent
- Somatic sensations (body aches and pains or numb)
- Goal is to become your own best resource and live in each moment fully.

W—Withdrawal

Not only are you withdrawing emotionally from your lost love, you are withdrawing physically from adrenaline. When we are attached/connected, our adrenaline level is elevated, when the attachment is broken, the level of adrenaline drops, we go through withdrawal physically because adrenaline is an addictive hormone. Anderson says, we may feel irritable, edgy, agitated, desperate, we may beg, manipulate, and crave. We become hypervigilant, having been wrenched apart, without security. There is a will to run riot, resulting in unpredictable behaviour. We cannot accept that we have no control over the separation or loss. We want a "fix." We find ourselves saying things like, "I will just call and say I have mail for them," or "maybe I will just drive by" or the phone rings, or a car pulls up, we start thinking, maybe it is them! In short, we get an adrenaline fix.

I—Internalizing the Rejection

We begin blaming ourselves for the rejection/abandonment, thinking, "I must have (or not have) said or done something." We idealize the abandoner; "he/she was so great!" We have Impotent rage. There is nothing to do with this rage. and nowhere to put it. As Anderson says, we experience isolation and shame, indictment, identity crises, invisibility. Keeping up the fight is an alternative to getting sick. Much research has been done to connect trauma and chronic illness. (ACES (Adverse Childhood Experiences))

R—Rage

Volatile rage is actually active resistance to being a victim. Yay! Ready to explode, reversing the rejection, renouncing the abandoner, reversing the loss, railing against reality, resentment, rewriting the ending, revamping the outside first, revenge (Anderson). This is the stage you take the energy created by the rage and heightened adrenaline and make a plan to keep yourself safe in the present and the future, i.e., "I will never let that happen again. I will do this instead." Thus, a plan is born.

L—Lifting

We begin to feel lighter, see light at the end of the tunnel, learn emotional lessons, lessening stress, and tension, healing from lost hopes and dreams, letting go of shame, lifting the barriers to finding love again, and letting go of the emotional bonds of the past (Anderson). There are, however, some pitfalls in this stage. We can lift right over top of our feelings instead of allowing ourselves time to experience the uncomfortableness of each stage and healing. Rebound relationships are one example of a pitfall of lifting.

These stages are not linear, and we can SWIRL through all stages in a few minutes and then back to the shattering stage again.

The abandonment stages, the archetypes, and scripture have many teachings that overlap and can complement each other, giving counsellors and others another way to view personal growth, relationships, and the world around them.

It is not our intent to "make" Christianity or scripture "fit" into the other two concepts; it is rather to demonstrate how scriptural precepts and concepts/teachings can manifest in psychological theories.

As I stated earlier, each chapter will begin with an explanation of the archetype, followed by how abandonment fits into that theory. We then share how scripture intersects with the archetype and abandonment. We finish each chapter with our own personal stories of how the archetype, abandonment, and scripture fits into our lives.

CHAPTER ONE
The Innocent
(Sharon)

I N THIS CHAPTER I will be discussing the Innocent and the Orphan as they pertain to the abandonment theory and scripture.

Goal of abandonment: To preserve some of the innocence that assists us in having plans and dreams. The goal is to not abandon this part of ourselves that we were born with.

The Innocent archetype, according to Carol Pearson (1986), is a state in which we all begin and where we can all return as we take our journey. When I speak of journey, I am referring to the act of taking our life experiences and situations and allowing them to be gifts to assist in our development and maturation, to assist us in becoming the person we were created to be. Thomas Moore (2017), in his book *Ageless Soul,* refers to this type of development as "aging" rather than growing older, becoming all of who we are as we age.

An archetype is not a destination or a place or state we arrive at and remain in for the rest of our lives (see Pearson, 1986, p. 6). This is true also for the stages of abandonment grief. Archetypes may be repeated/revisited many times as our journey through life unfolds. Certain archetypes may be our default coping mechanism, the one we unconsciously use during times of internal stress. The archetype we default to is dependent upon which emotion or body memory is activated by an external stimulus or what the need is in any given situation. For example, a feeling being activated might be, "I am afraid and need someone to help me, rescue me." The emotion I would be feeling here is fear, and the belief is that I cannot take care of myself. If I am in such a situation in a work setting and I hold the belief that a role my supervisor has is to protect me in various situations, and when that does not happen, I can easily default to the Orphan state as a response, back to parents who did not protect me and a teacher who betrayed me. That is the Orphan archetype being activated. In the beginning, the Innocent is very trusting, such as in the first blissful, rose-coloured glasses stage of love. In this state, we accept wholeheartedly what we see, never questioning or even being aware that other characteristics may lie outside our realm of awareness. This is the state we want things/life to remain in forever, and we may believe it will remain so.

This state can become a recurring theme. The notion, idea, or belief that needs will always be met without any effort from us can create difficulty in adult relationships. The difficulty arises when the belief is carried into the workplace, our intimate relationships, friendships, and or family. Looking through those rose-coloured glasses of the Innocent, we are unaware that we have responsibilities in relationships and that other people or situations are perhaps not as we see them or experience them. An example of this is the perception that "I will find 'my person', then I will be looked after"—Sleeping Beauty waiting for her prince to rescue her.

In abandonment theory, the Innocent can be seen in Little, the internal child/the child within all of us. This emotional/mental state is Little before the rose-coloured glasses came off before Little was abandoned in some way and fear became a reality. It is an infant whose needs are met, and even though there may be some upsets, the bliss state is returned to quickly. Yet paradoxically, the first abandonment is the rejection from the womb. If the birth is traumatic in some way, this leaves a trauma body memory as well as a rejection body memory (The

Body Keeps the Score (2014) van der Kolk, Bessel). The act of being born can be long and painful, and then you are in the bright lights, a cool room, and perhaps smacked to start breathing. The caregivers of an infant would have to be more than exceptional for an infant to not experience abandonment while in the first hours of life. Being put in a bassinet, crying for even a couple of minutes, and being cold and hungry are all ways that set up a template for distrust. We cannot escape childhood.

Again, we experience this state in beginning romances. We see what we want to believe is the whole truth. Then as time goes by, we experience reality, which will be discussed in the Orphan stage.

In Christianity, the Innocent would be a pre-fallen state, Grace. It is the Garden of Eden where all needs have been taken care of before there was even a felt need. In this state, there is always someone to meet our needs. In the Garden of Eden, it was God. In this state, we have our needs met by Grace, and by acknowledging and revering other and self.

THE ORPHAN

This archetype may manifest in various ways. I think it is important to remember this is a journey, and to have compassion as we search for new ways to be taken care of and survive.

Goal of the Orphan: To find safety and self reliance.

Goal of Little in abandonment: to be safe and looked after. Little learns to rely on themselves. Both Little and Orphan fear abandonment.

The Orphan is the archetype that learns/teaches us how to live in a world where needs may not be met when we need or expect them to be met. The world after Innocence is the world of reality. The Orphan is distrusting of everything and everyone; Little is always on guard for the next disappointment and the next powerless situation.

The task of the Orphan is to survive. A goal of the Orphan archetype is to find someone to care for them, to keep them safe, to seek out and find a return to the Innocent. Another task of the Orphan is to learn to admit when they need help. The need to be looked after can sometimes be perceived, by the self and others as being needy, demanding, or having entitlement issues.

ABANDONMENT IN THE ORPHAN ARCHETYPE

In abandonment theory, Little can become very fearful and distrust everything and everyone, especially ourselves. This fear activates the survival part of the brain known as the amygdala which triggers a flood of adrenaline and cortisol to help us survive. Little feels very much like an orphan in such a scenario: unsafe, with no one to trust or to help them.

In this part of the abandonment theory, one of the learnings is to be able to separate the past and the present. Feelings from past losses are activated when there is a potential for loss in the present. These past feelings become entangled with feelings arising from the present situation, creating a sometimes-overwhelming sense of loss. We need a way to reduce the adrenaline and experience only those feelings truly arising from the present situation. One tool to help us be in the present moment and reduce the flooding of adrenaline is to activate our senses; ask yourself, "What do I see, hear, smell, taste, feel by touch?" We cannot be in our senses and emotions at the same time. They reside in different parts of our brain. We become regulated, calmer, more able to be present and so we are then less defended when we activate our senses.

These are easy words to say and a seemingly simple enough concept. What I know to be true is it is an ongoing learning process to be present with ourselves in the here and now. This state of consciousness takes work, and it can be challenging to be able to expand the tension container to tolerate the uncomfortableness. It is impossible to be present all the time. This is only one tool to help regulate our nervous system. There are many tools offered on YouTube by therapists such as Bessel Van der Kolk, Peter Levine, and Stephen Porges, to name a few.

SWIRL

Shattering

I think for each archetype we experience the SWIRL of abandonment theory; some for a longer and perhaps more intense time. There is a shattering that takes place in the Innocent to activate the Orphan archetype. We become shattered when we realize what we thought or believed is not actually the way things are. When we believe we have been betrayed by friends, family, authority figures, when needs and expectations are not met, we experience a shattering of the trust we held in them and in ourselves, becoming doubtful of our abilities and capabilities. We think things like, "Well, I made that decision, I chose that person, and I was wrong, again. I will never get it right." Self-doubt is one of the major components of abandonment. Self-doubt keeps us in an internal conflict, and that way we can keep all the patterns the same, which loops us back to Little not trusting us to make healthy, protecting decisions.

The goal of the shattering stage is to learn how to be our own best resource (Anderson), which means to be the one who looks after our own needs, to be the adult the Orphan and Little are seeking. As explained above, going to our senses allows us to be in the part of our brain that reasons. It is in this executive functioning part of our brain that we can figure out what our needs are and how to meet them.

Being our own best resource also includes learning how to ask for help and admitting when we are not able to do any more or when we have reached our limit, whether that be emotionally, mentally, spiritually, or financially. It is saying/knowing that we have exhausted our own resources. This is a healthy awareness on the healing journey.

Withdrawal

In the withdrawal stage of abandonment, we are no longer attached to the external object, whether that be the lost partner, job, or friend. The attachment has been broken or changed in some significant way. When we are no longer attached, there is a void in our heart/soul/inner being. We seek to fill the void, so we work more, drink more, take drugs, or find another relationship. We may even return to the one who shattered our dreams and plans. We medicate away our pain and disillusionment, whether literally or figuratively.

Engaging in activities that raise our adrenaline is part of the withdrawal stage. We are without the object we were attached to, and we are also experiencing a decrease in adrenaline, which is addictive (The Journey from Abandonment to Healing (2000) Anderson, Susan). We look for the heart's desire, pinning our hope on someone or something outside ourselves—anything or anyone to lessen the tension-riddled experience of withdrawal.

Each time we have a new encounter with someone who does stick by us, we have an opportunity to heal, and we increase our trust a little more to heal and gain emotional maturity, Orphan and Little come to understand and accept that the initial shattering or fall was not all their doing. They come to accept that they are not responsible for someone else's actions or decisions.

Internalizing the Rejection

As the Orphan, we internalize the disappointment or disillusionment experienced in the shattering stage. We self-blame. Depending on the scenario, we may ask ourselves questions like, "What did I do?" "How come this rejection/shattering is happening to me?" "How come no one is helping me?" "Why didn't my supervisor step in?" We feel victimized and alone. Through internalizing and self-blame, we can turn ourselves inside out to "make" the other person happy, or (people please) fawn. We so want to get it "right" so we will not be rejected or abandoned.

The behaviour coming out of this part of our brain (amygdala) is reactionary rather than response based. Reactionary behaviour is perpetrated by Chuckee, the Outer Child. The doll "Chucky" killed people, and the Chuckee in abandonment theory kills any chance for change or true intimacy. As stated earlier, Chuckee's job is to take Little's fear away and keep all the behavioural patterns the same. These reactions keep us stuck in the Orphan archetype. Change for Little is a fear-filled place because it leads to unknown elements. This is a loop behaviour. Little and Orphan want to be looked after, so they find someone and then experience a flood of fear that at some point they will be abandoned. Thus, they revert to old familiar patterns of behaviour, such as fawning. Little and Orphan would have to change and mature to stay in a trusting relationship.

As a young child, the only way to make sense of other's behaviours or situations or have any control is to internalize the meaning of these situations and actions. We believe we can perhaps stay safe if we change our behaviour.

Rage

The rage stage of abandonment allows us to feel anger, undo the internalizing, and make plans for safety using the energy from anger. Anger energy is great fuel for productivity and change, and it also comes with negative elements that must be processed.

Anger, for Little and the Orphan, can be expressed as blame. It is easier (less fearful, more familiar) to blame others than it is to change or embrace our own responsibility for situations. Underlying the rage is fear, which could also be fear of the rage, and so we sometimes suppress that feeling. Rage also stems from the fear of rejection and loss. Instead of processing anger, Chuckee will manipulate, seduce, or coerce to get needs met without having to change or show the rage.

Some people believe that if they let go of their rage that some how they are saying the abuse, oppression, or whatever the case may be was not big enough, painful enough, or legitimate enough to hang onto. They have become identified by their story/pain. This thinking also keeps the Orphan stuck. One of the ways Chuckee keeps change in check is by comparing trauma wounds with the trauma wounds of others and holding on to past wounds. Thus, in some way, it legitimizes holding on to the pain/trauma pattern. As we learn how to manage rage in a healthier way, we see opportunities to emerge into a less painful way of being. This seeing new ways of being is part of lifting.

Lifting

Lifting plays a part in both Orphan and Little. Little experiences positive change situations when the adult self (Big) can stand in without becoming defensive (Chuckee). The adult part of us can feel fear and remain adult and in the frontal lobe part of our brain. These experiences, when made conscious, enthuse Little with a sense of trust in the adult self's ability to manage self and feelings in situations and relationships. Orphan has an experience of finding someone to look after them and feel safe. Both Little and Orphan can then take the steps to mature and move forward.

HOW DO FAITH AND GOD'S WORD INTERSECT WITH THE ORPHAN ARCHETYPE? (KATHY)

"God spoke: 'Let us make human beings in our image, make them, reflecting our nature. So, they can be responsible for the fish in the sea, the birds in the air, the cattle, And, yes, Earth itself, and every animal that moves on the face of Earth.' God created human beings; he created them godlike, Reflecting God's nature. He created them male and female. God blessed them: 'Prosper! Reproduce! Fill Earth! Take charge! Be responsible for fish in the sea and birds in the air, for every living thing that moves on the face of Earth.'"

—Genesis 1:26–28

What a beautiful picture of the peace and beauty of Eden and creation! God said be free and flourish, and that's what the Innocent does! However, our lives cannot reflect the innocence of Eden forever. We don't want to think of it and certainly can't plan for it or understand it, but pain will enter our lives. Pain of any kind might bounce us from the bliss of the Innocent to the pain of the Orphan. However, God will not leave us in this place alone. God is always walking along with us (Psalm 23). He holds us up (Isaiah 10:41) and shapes us (Isaiah 64:8), teaches us the skills we need to walk the next part of the journey (Proverbs 6:23). These verses and many others help us to endure the pain and loneliness of the Orphan.

Though difficult to accept and not pleasant to think about, at some point we can no longer close our eyes and ignore man's imperfect love and care for one another. At some point in our lives, somebody or some circumstance will not meet our expectations. This is where we meet the Orphan archetype. This is where I feel the most loneliness, the most disconnection and separation from the world.

I think we all react differently, but this is when I often look to others around me and hope they will see me in this place and help me by lifting and rescuing me from my circumstances. I have learned that no one can rescue me. I need to rescue myself by reaching out for God and discovering and obeying His Word in the Bible. He is always waiting for me to give me solace, strength, love, and understanding. One verse has sustained me through thick and thin, Isaiah 41:10: "So do not fear, for I am with you; do not be dismayed, for I am your God. I will strengthen you and help you; I will uphold you with my righteous right hand." No matter what happens in life, God is there to hold me up and keep me close. I am not alone. I am constantly reassured in God's Word that I am not a spiritual orphan: "Be strong and courageous. Do not be afraid or terrified because of them, for the Lord your God goes with you; he will never leave you nor forsake you" (Deuteronomy 31:6).

God will never abandon me even if those I love and who I thought loved me most desert me. God is my "strength and my shield" (Psalm 28:7) from the tumultuous circumstances of my life and the world around me. While growing through the Orphan archetype, with God's help, I can learn to trust myself again because I know He loves me (Psalm 136:26) and He created me just the way I am (Isaiah 64:8). I can learn to face the reality of the world, the good and the bad in people and in circumstances. I have learned that the pain of the Orphan can be transformative, a tool to compel learning and promote strength:

> Even youths grow tired and weary, and young men stumble
> and fall; but those who hope in the Lord will renew their
> strength. They will soar on wings like eagles; they will run
> and not grow weary; they will walk and not be faint.
>
> (Isaiah 40:30–31)

Kathy's Personal Experience of the "Orphan" Archetype

Sometimes, when I take time to self-reflect, I think I have been stuck in the Orphan or Altruist archetype for most of my life. They both are very recurrent themes for me and evidence themselves often. My first experience with the Orphan was at three or four years of age.

Even as a child, I treasured the outdoors. I loved to feel the cool green grass beneath my feet, watch the plants growing day by day, listen to the sounds of the birds in the garden, smell the earth and the different fragrances of plants. I loved it all! My favourite song was "The Man on the Flying Trapeze." It spoke to me of freedom! My favourite pastime as a little girl was making mud pies with my friend (also named Kathy) who lived next door. We would play for hours mixing the mud, finding the perfect mix of dirt and water, catching worms for decoration (not healthy for the worms, I realize now), and as a final touch, sprinkling our cakes with bits of grass or twigs. Those are happy memories! My needs were met. I was content and ensconced in the Innocent archetype.

I was about four years old when my mom was pregnant with my little sister. It was an exciting time, but also very fearful for me. My mom was not well and was soon confined to bed. Dad was at work every day to support the family and my older sister was off to high school with a life of her own. During the day it was just me and Mom. I remember thinking that I was taking care of her, and I was terrified of what might happen to Mom or the baby if I did not care for her correctly. I took our lunch from the fridge every day, taking Mom's into her bedroom and placing the dirty dishes in the sink afterwards. I was reminded daily of the little flag near the window because if we needed help, it was my job to put the flag in the window so that our neighbour would see it and come to help us. At four years old, I checked for it often and rehearsed in my mind just what to do.

There was a small patch of grass just outside Mom's bedroom window. That was my play area. I was not allowed to venture outside that area because that patch of grass was the extent of Mom's vision from her bedside window. I was terrified of putting even a foot where it should not be for fear my naughty behaviour would upset my mom and make her "sicker." In consequence, this was the end of my mud pie passion because Kathy's house and the "sand" box were on the opposite side of my play area. I was trapped, and I have found myself in that trapped place repeatedly since then! My perception is that repeatedly, I have been trapped in different types of relationships, in work situations, in volunteer positions, in illness—trapped and afraid to move beyond my current circumstances.

When my first marriage failed, I found myself learning to live life differently with two young children, a seven-year-old and a three-year-old. My ex-husband was working overseas. Money was tight and life was stressful. I would not trade one day with my children for anything in the world; however, because of the single mother lifestyle, day-to-day living often consisted of doing everything for other people and very little for myself. I began to lose touch with who I am at the core of my soul. I was staying in the safe play space of the Orphan, afraid to venture into the world on my own. Single parenthood is demanding and carving out time for yourself is almost impossible. I needed to find space and the help of a counselor to heal and move through the Orphan Archetype. What I know now is that I was meeting my needs by meeting the needs of others and making sure they were emotionally okay.

Three years later, I met someone that encouraged me to be my own person, to break free. Reluctantly, I started on a personal journey, a quest to live my life outside the expectations of others. The process was gradual and seemingly inconsequential at first. When we went out together in the evening, if we were taking my car, he insisted that I drive. Unbelievably, that was the first tiny step towards a renewed sense of self. Soon I realized that in relationship with my family, I had once again started to make decisions that were right for me and the kids but not necessarily in line with the expectations of others. I was beginning to experience freedom again.

Since then, in life's journey, I have slipped back into and replayed this pattern many times, in relationships and in the workplace. I may continue to do so, but when I catch myself feeling trapped and afraid, I immediately, with God's help, begin to take baby steps to freedom:

> For God gave us a spirit not of fear but of power and love and self-control
>
> (2 Timothy 1:7).

SHARON'S PERSONAL EXPERIENCE OF THE ORPHAN ARCHETYPE

Due to my many abandonment experiences from a very early age, I can return to the Orphan archetype quite quickly and often. When we have had a traumatic experience, we unconsciously set up situations that mirror that experience so we can change it and heal the wound from that original trauma. This pattern of behaviour shares a name with Bessel van der Kolk's (1989) article on the topic, "The Compulsion to Repeat the Trauma."

I projected my fears of being abandoned onto partners, authority figures, and especially employers. Growing up, neither parent was capable of protecting me from the other one or any external threat. Wanting to be protected and looked after, wanting fairness between siblings, I found myself teaching them (my parents), in childlike ways, about fairness, morals, parenting, and was rewarded with my mother sarcastically calling me Mahatma Gandhi! I thought my mother was swearing at me until I was much older and learned who Gandhi was and what he stood for.

I was about nine years old when this name-calling started. I realized much later in life that it was at this age when I was beginning to find my voice and my mother did not like it. Unconsciously, I was probably delighting in levelling the playing field. I knew my mother would be angry, and I then had some power.

All I ever wanted was for an adult to "get it" and rescue me. I was in my forties before I really understood what was probably happening with my mother. I think I was mirroring a part of her she could not access in herself, the part that could name what was happening and find the courage to make the change in her own life. As a child, what I knew from my experience was, nothing I said or did ever effected change in anything. If anything, I would get even more rejected, and at times I wondered if I was adopted. The message I internalized was, if they would just "get it," I would be safe—hence me trying to teach my parents. If they didn't know how to change their behaviour, to be less abusive and to be more protective, then I would teach them. How presumptuous of me! However, all that behaviour was totally unconscious and a response of the Orphan, of Little, to get my needs met.

In my older teen years and as an adult, I would choose partners who in the beginning, seemed secure and protective, just like my parents until I was nine months old. Relationships would be emotional roller coasters. All or nothing thinking, push and pull, come here, go away, I love you, I hate you. I did not know how to love any better than my parents did.

Employers were my biggest "gift" of unconscious repeats. Everything would start out roses, then a situation would arise which I would interpret as not being protected by my employer, and they would "fall". I became the fear-filled Little and an Orphan. Chuckee would start a mental tirade about not being able to trust them and how we needed to resign, quit, run away. After a couple of these very painful experiences, I twigged to what I was re-creating. So, I turned it around and told myself, Sharon, "If you would only 'get it' that these people do not need to 'get it' for you to be safe, you would be able to keep yourself safe." This hyper-sensitivity to rejection is now being called a trauma response.

Freedom! It is easy to put this into practice. Have I repeated that cycle again since that revelation? Of course, I have. The last couple of times I have recognized the pattern much quicker. In the last re-creation, I found myself educating the employer as a way to facilitate change. In sharing my experience with my friend, I became conscious of another part of the re-creation. I never understood or was even conscious of the fact that what I had been doing as a child was educating my parents. It is not a child's job to educate the parents. It is not my job to educate employers out of my feelings of fear. I am not three or nine years old, others are not my parents, and I can look after myself now. I can leave or stay as I choose which I was not free to do as a child. Will I re-create the Orphan again? I do not know. My guess is probably. However, hopefully it happens in a healthier way. Is there more I can learn from this re-creation? Perhaps. I do not need to know. What I do know is I do not have to remain in Little or the Orphan state unless I choose.

I think this next example is important to share because I believe it illustrates a time in my Orphan life when I was my own best resource. Well, it was probably a God intervention. When I was couch surfing as a young teen—thirteen, fourteen years old—and I ran out of couches to crash on, I would become very ill. I manifested elevated temperature, stomach/abdominal pain, and achy joints. I would go to the emergency room, and I would be admitted. I was unconscious of the fact I was making myself ill to have a place to sleep because it was winter and cold. Also, exams were upcoming, and because of work and being in survival mode, I was not a stellar student in Grade Nine. Being sick and in hospital meant I avoided failing the exams. I could then say I failed the year because I had been sick and in hospital. For more information about body/somatic manifestations research ACES adverse childhood experiences.

Looking back, I am perplexed in how that all came together. To my knowledge, my parents never knew I was in the hospital, and no one at the hospital ever asked me where I lived. I do not think my mother signed me in or was even notified. In my forties, when my mother and I shared some of our experiences around my life and I told her about the hospital episodes, she was not aware of them.

I think this demonstrates the Orphan and Little reaching out for help in the only way they knew how to, knowing they could not do it on their own, risking and trusting that somehow, they would be looked after, building a small foundation of trust. My doctor knew my home life, and I always thought/believed he was responsible for ensuring I was admitted and safe. Perhaps he was one of God's ministering angels.

Today when the Orphan stage is being resurrected and I feel sick suddenly, I pay attention and examine what is going on in my life. Is there something I want to avoid/get out of? Do I want/need to be taken care of? Where am I not taking care of myself/what is my need? I can now re-create a time of safety in a matter of seconds. What was safety then, however, now only serves to keep me stuck in the Orphan archetype waiting for a rescuer. This is a clue for me that I have abandoned a need somewhere along my journey. I could have abandoned myself yesterday or last week. As I heal, the timeline for recognizing my self-abandonment patterns shortens.

Another example of projecting my needs for my parents to protect me can be seen in the following experience. Beginning in Grade Five, the principal of the school began to molest me as well as many other girls, touching breasts and looking up skirts when he would ask the girls to climb a ladder or swing higher on the swing. A group of us girls would walk together down the hall with our arms wrapped around each other so he could not squeeze his hand between our arms and breasts. Unconsciously, we knew everyone knew. One day, a group of us girls left the school grounds at lunch time and walked to our favourite teacher's home. We explained to her what was happening, and as we were talking to her, she was slowly closing the door, and abruptly ended the conversation with, "I am sorry I cannot help you." We were all dismayed. For me, this betrayal has lasted a lifetime. I knew the teacher had a role and a responsibility to protect students, and I also wanted her to care enough about me to protect me.

School was my safe place. Home was abusive and non-supportive, so school was the place I wanted to be. I really admired this teacher who seemed supportive and caring. When she refused to help, rescue, support or even have compassion, I realize now I shut down. I continued at that school for another two years and the teacher never spoke about what happened. She pretended nothing was ever said to her. This is when my anger began to surface. I wasn't aware I was angry; I just knew that I wasn't safe anywhere now and I had to protect myself. I projected all my thoughts and beliefs about women in authority onto my female superiors. They were not to be trusted and I believed I was stronger than they were.

Another recurring example is in past years, when I would be out for a walk, I would get these thoughts that if I looked in the bush or the ditch, I would discover an abandoned baby. Freaky for sure. As I did my healing work, I uncovered my belief that I was thrown away as a baby and that I was searching for myself/seeking to find that lost baby part of me. I still have that sudden body sensation from time to time while walking. It is another clue that I have abandoned myself somewhere in my journey or I am seeking to find another part of myself. This experience is now met with gratitude that I am healing. God is great and not finished with me yet.

SHARON'S PERSONAL EXPERIENCES OF SCRIPTURAL TEACHING ON THE ORPHAN

"God wants to gather His children as a mother
hen would gather her chicks…"
—Luke 13:34

"…because I rescued the poor who cried for help, and
the fatherless who had none to assist them."
—Job 29:12

"My peace I give to you, not as the world gives do I give to
you. Let not your heart be troubled, neither let it be afraid."
—John 14:27

The first time I heard that scripture I experienced shackles and callouses falling away from my heart; for the first time, it did not matter if my dad loved me or not, I had a father! I wanted to shout it from the rooftops.

Many scripture verses come to mind that aptly describe my experiences when I think about my time in the Orphan archetype.

As I shared earlier in the chapter, my father was abusive, and my mother did not protect me, and school began to mirror that experience, so I really was an orphan spiritually, mentally, emotionally, and physically. I was the only girl among four brothers and was also the middle child. Now, one might suppose I would have been given everything my heart desired. Wrong. I was everything my brothers were not. I spoke about morals and ethics. I told the truth, I helped the neighbours, I looked after neighbours' kids, and I did the cleaning and the cooking. I was employed from the time I was thirteen and helped to buy food at home or helped with bills when I lived there. My mother knew nothing of my giving Dad money to pay bills until I was in my twenties. I think for her by this time it was a mirror, another failure as a mother in her mind.

I remember when we moved to Ontario from a farm in Manitoba, we bought a house. I was ten. My brother and I rode our bikes to the house to wait for Mom, Dad, the other kids, and the delivery truck. I was so sure I was at the right house—a cute little two-storey white house with blue trim and a fence (anyone see the Innocent here?). When Mom and Dad arrived, I was so excited to have them unlock the door. A room of my own! None of us had bedrooms in our home in Manitoba.

But wait . . . Mom and Dad went to the wrong house, didn't they? Why did they go to a really small house with no white fence and one storey? I went in, and I must have walked through the house four or five times searching for the third bedroom. Finally, I asked Mom where my room was. She looked at me like I had three heads. I said, "Where am I going to sleep?" She kept looking at me like she had forgotten I might need that. In exasperation, she flung out, "On the couch, I guess."

Needless to say, I was crushed. I was so hurt I yelled at her that I didn't know why they bought the house when there was no room for me. I also asked accusingly, if they couldn't look after me, why did they have me? With that, I left the house and rode around on my bike until dark. When I returned, no one asked where I had been or if I was alright. That incident captures the message I interpreted as a child. I was not wanted. I had no room, and the expectation was to need in silence. Thrown away again.

So, now that I have given some background, I want to share another story, an experience that took place when I was three. It was evening just after supper. I know I was three because my younger brother was a tiny baby; he was born in January, and I was born in December three years apart. My dad had slapped me across the face just before supper. He did this in front of my mother, who was standing at the stove stirring gravy. She did not miss a beat from stirring, nor did she look at me or say anything. I remember being shocked and refusing to cry. I wanted to run away. I put on a snowsuit and boots and went out. No one stopped me or asked where I was going (this pattern carries over throughout my life).

It was dusk, and the stars were just beginning to peek out and twinkle—my favourite time. I walked down our fairly long driveway (to a three-year-old) and across the road and sat on a very high solid bank of snow. I looked up at the stars and the sky and said, "Well, God, it's just me and you."

What did a farm kid know about God? But somewhere inside, I knew. The experience was spirit to spirit, deep to deep. I knew God was with me, even though I could not put it into words. I had also learned I could not count on either parent for help or safety. This experience plays over in my mind, reminding me I am never alone.

I know I can rest in Him, count on Him, trust Him. I know that even when I walked away and came back, He had His arms wide open and has given me back the years the locusts ate (Joel 2:25).

While I know and believe this to be true and that it holds enormous healing value in my life, coming to a place of trust and acceptance has been a journey fraught with giving and taking. I give my problems and worries to God and take them back, I take His trust I give it back, I take His forgiveness and give it back. Psalm 85:8–13 tells us we can expect good things from the Lord; well, this is where the rubber meets the road because that is very foreign to my experience and my beliefs about love. Joy is difficult to experience when I am used to something bad happening, so I do not get too excited about anything because I expect someone will take it away. I learned to take it away from myself first (Chuckee) However, I continue to learn and take the leap of faith, allowing healing to happen.

I also had an amazing therapist who saw me through about ten years of therapy. She was so quiet and unassuming, she held space for me and let me fill that space with my emerging self. I am forever grateful to Susan Breiddal.

I have many experiences of being in the Orphan archetype and just as many experiences of scripture leading me out and reassuring me that I am never alone and that I have value and purpose no matter what my condition or circumstance. When I was preparing to give my testimony, I wrote this song:

One Set of Footprints

I was just a little girl
Alone in a great big world.
I needed a mama to keep me safe,
To wrap me in her arms,
Take away my fears,
But all that I ever got were just more tears.
I awoke with a start
In the middle of the night
With a hand over my mouth to silence my fright.
Alone and confused
I cried silently,
GOD, WHY ME?
Well, I wandered through the years
Masking all my fears
Looking for answers from everyone I met.
Won't you please comfort me,
Tell me I'm okay
But all that I ever had was just more pain.
Someone said He's there, but I didn't know where.
But there was a hole deep inside me where I knew love should be.
So, I was still all alone, crying silently,
God, why me? God, why me?
(Instrumental and talking)

Well, you know He really was there all the time, and when I changed "God, why me?" Into "God, save me," a miracle happened. Yes, I'm a miracle. He picked me up and began to restore my mind and mend my broken heart. He turned my life around. You know, I often wondered why I hadn't made some choices and why I had done some things.

Well, one day God showed me the reason, and as I looked, the words to that poem flashed through my mind because what I saw was one set of footprints. My heart breaks and my eyes fill when I think of all the love He has always had for me and how I hurt Him so much. Yes, He's filling that empty place where love should have always been, and His love heals my wounds. I feel confused sometimes by all that love because it is not something I am used to, and, well, at times, I don't know what to do. My prayer, though, is that some of it will spill over onto you, and you can get to know Him, and then you too will see the times in your life when there was only

One set of footprints.

God, thank YOU.

My granddaughter drew this for me and gave me permission to use it in the book. I hope it conveys some of the essence of what this time may have been like for me.

CHAPTER TWO

The Martyr/Altruist
(Sharon)

ELVING INTO THE Martyr/Altruist Archetype can uncover hidden aspects of ourselves. Depending on how wounded we are, or how healed we are, we can find ourselves being very kind and generous one moment and defended and mean in the next moment. Awareness is part of the journey of the Martyr/Altruist that points to areas we could choose to change.

Goal of the Martyr/Altruist: To know that you are good enough.

Goal of Abandonment: To understand that you are always looked after when you are connected to self and others. To know you always have and are enough.

I struggle with this archetype. I have sat down to write a few times and have discovered other things that I suddenly decide need doing right now! This avoidance is a red flag telling me there is a huge learning in this archetype for me. I am uncertain as to the nature of the teaching; however, what I do know is I do not like who I become in the face of a toxic martyr.

A toxic Martyr is an "over the edge" Martyr, one who has slipped into the Orphan/victim archetype. I almost instantly become Chuckee, and in my mind, I say to the other, "You want to be a victim? Let me help you." My behaviour is probably experienced as one of non-acceptance, rejection, and very little compassion. I become the Martyr/victim, Little; I abandon myself. Great projection. I will write more about this in my personal experiences of Martyr archetype. As with all archetypes, there is another side to the Martyr/Altruist. This archetype can display heartfelt acts of service and can be genuine and humble. Suffice it to say, I am struggling as I write this.

As Carol Pearson (1986) says in her book, the meaning of the term martyr has changed over the years. At one time, it meant to freely give of the self to the point of sacrifice/suffer, if necessary, one who would lay down their life for a friend. Carol Pearson has changed her archetype name to the Altruist. So, I am using both. Today the term Martyr represents someone who is very dramatic in their giving of themselves. The sacrifice is hurting them, and they want you to know how much they hurt. In reality, they are not truly selflessly giving of self; it is a pseudo-martyrish behaviour. This behaviour is manipulative and has many strings attached.

I find this behaviour much like that of the victim; the "giving" is a duty, a need to meet either an internal or external expectation. The unconscious dialogue of the Martyr may sound like, "If I were caring, I should want to do this and this and this." They may genuinely want to take on a caregiver role, and it lasts until they don't want to anymore, and then Chuckee reacts. Chuckee sabotages the Martyr's good works by reacting to Little's fear of becoming suffocated by the other person's needs. This is a fear of putting boundaries in place for self-protection.

Attached to this behaviour is a belief that we must give and sacrifice in order to earn something and also prove something (our worthiness). When we do not receive that which we have been working toward earning, we become frustrated and perhaps resentful.

When I am working with people, one of the things I teach (correctly or incorrectly) is that we never do anything for anyone else. I know this is contrary to the teachings in some parts of scripture;

however, I believe it to be true. When I am working with clients, I ask them to name one thing they have done for their children. I usually have to stop them as a whole litany of good deeds is strung out. When I posit that perhaps they did all those things because they believed that is what a "good" parent did, they agreed whole heartedly. So, then the following question is, who has a need to be a good parent? Had they ever had the experience of saying to their teen, "After all I have done for you, you won't even . . ." The teen frequently responds with, "I never asked you to."

When you can begin to understand that everything we do comes from our own needs, beliefs, or desires, then there aren't any strings attached and therefore no resentments. True need comes from an internal locus and is not defined by an external requirement. The journey, then, becomes one of self-awareness regarding discernment. A question I ask myself is, "Am I acting/doing from a place of true service (love) or is this behaviour an old, ingrained pattern, and I am doing what is familiar without being aware of the origin? Am I acting out of love or am I acting out of fear that has become habituated?"

We cannot always remain in any archetype, no matter what our ideals are. As we journey and heal, we have more emotional surface (Anderson, 2000) which allows us to attach to others and ourselves. I am extrapolating that we therefore can have more and quicker access to the archetypes which would assist us in a well way in any given situation. In abandonment terms, we can access our frontal lobe and respond rather than react with Chuckee behaviour after we have done the work of healing.

The Martyr/Altruist, in its intended form, is a journey of learning to serve in a healthy way. It is about embracing the suffering of life's journey and the suffering that comes from giving at one's own expense. It is an expression of genuine love and caring. The need in our self to meet other's needs is very strong and can become sometimes a defining part of who we are in the world.

Abandonment in
the Martyr Archetype

The Martyr archetype abandons self and other when they are not being truthful with themselves or the other about the agenda driving their actions. Perhaps the agenda is deeply unconscious and has become the preferred or the familiar way to act with the root motivator being buried in the unconscious.

The Martyr also abandons by returning to the Orphan archetype when serving does not elicit the end results desired. This behaviour may manifest as the victim, wanting to be praised, rescued, or acknowledged. This is an example of giving with strings attached.

The toxic part of the Martyr becomes a very codependent, unconsciously controlling type person. This is a learned behaviour based on survival when experiencing emotional threats, whether real or imagined. One way to understand codependent behaviour is to remember that it is about emotional safety. The codependent person thinks that the only way they are emotionally safe is if the "other" is experiencing safe feelings like happy or joyful or caring emotions. The codependent person will manipulate to control for those emotions by such behaviours as lying ("well I just won't say I spent all that money because if he knows, he will be upset") or another manipulation to stay emotionally safe could be, ("I will cook favourite foods and he will forget to blame me"). This is manipulative and controlling to elicit only certain behaviours.

The true Martyr or Altruist can abandon self when we miss the inner voice guiding us. When we put off acting/doing/being in a way that we know we are called to, we abandon ourselves and others.

The gift of discernment is required to know the difference between true service and familiar patterning. There is also a need to understand that we need self-care and balance. While true service can fill the soul, there is need for serving the self in practical ways: time outs, time alone, time to accept being served. When we fail to recognize our basic human needs, we run the risk of abandoning ourselves.

SWIRL

Shattering

We become shattered when we realize that no matter how much we sacrifice to earn approval, acceptance, love, and self-worth, we still do not have those things. Our beliefs are on the chopping block; our hope is shattered. We are shocked that people are treating us in a manner that implies there needs to be a change. When we do not get the desired outcome from all we do and the message is clear, we understand change is looming and we will be confronting old patterns and belief systems.

We can also become shattered when we realize we missed an opportunity to serve. Sometimes we have an idea or image of ourselves as a Martyr or Altruist and then we realize perhaps that image is inaccurate. What happens to our image? The true Altruist/Martyr, however, does not have an image of self; it is a compelling calling/need.

Withdrawal

When we change patterns, we may lose some relationships. We also experience the washed out, tired, and weary feeling of always doing, always giving, and never receiving enough to have the void filled. We can also experience depression in this state of change. When we are depressed, we withdraw and isolate.

When we are in a healthy martyr/altruist archetype, we still deal with our human side, which wants things to be fair and or equal. Part of the journey is to remind ourselves to stay the course, recognize and be aware of the grieving process, steming from any loss, whether it be job, relationship, or death. A true Martyr/Altruist takes care of others as well as self.

Internalizing

In this stage we tell ourselves to "try" harder, do more, sacrifice more; then we will earn or receive the love we think we deserve, or whatever the case may be. This is the self-blame, which can turn into other-blaming and acting out in frustration and resentment. If we chose to take the journey of change, it is in this stage that we face a type of identity crises. If I am not a Martyr/Altruist, and that role does not serve me, then who am I, and what purpose do I have? In this stage, we can learn to make a true connection with ourselves and learn the lesson/task of how to serve from the heart.

Rage

In the toxic part of the Martyr, rage is frustration of not having the rewards of our sacrifices returned. Frustration is also a product of envy. I want what you have and yet I am the one not letting myself have whatever it is. In this envy place, one can act angry. The dark side of envy is destruction—if I can't have it, I will in some way destroy it for you as well. The rage may also be against the fear of change, the fear of facing shame, fear of facing our true self.

There is also a fear accompanying the idea of serving and sacrificing. When we come from scarcity, the fear of giving can sometimes seem insurmountable. Perhaps it seems our whole life as a child has been about sacrifice, and that was painful, so we do not want to repeat the experience. We rage against knowing that giving is the "right" thing to do.

Rage is also the state when we can use the energy to make a plan to carry out change, to take the Wanderer journey (which will be further described in the next chapter) to discover who we are as a true Martyr/

Altruist. This is a time to learn to embrace the joy of serving and sacrificing, as well as learning to balance it with care for the self. We enter a journey of unhooking old fears from today's wonderful opportunities.

Lifting

This is a time of learning to let go of ego identity that does not serve us anymore. We have come through the shame and the pain of realizing our actions have been self-serving out of fear and can now embrace and discover new ways of serving.

One of the fears of letting go and serving comes from a mistaken belief that if I let go of all my wounds and hurts that what I am saying is they didn't matter, they were not that bad, and they were not important. When we let go it is not that we forget, or the incidences were not painful, it is that we are saying they happened, and they no longer have control or power over us. Those things happened to me they are not who I am. There is a time for accepting reality and moving forward in our healing.

So, with all our feelings intact, and the lessons and experiences we have had, we lift and rise to embrace another way of being, one that can give to the self as well as freely give to the other.

Sharon's Personal Experience of the Martyr Archetype

I mentioned in the beginning of writing this chapter that I was struggling. Well, I still am. Perhaps I do not want to own this part of me because I am barely able to name it. I know I become Chuckee or as I sometimes call that part of me, my Inner Dorothy, referring to Dorothy from the Golden Girls (I know, I am dating myself). Dorothy's character was a passive-aggressive, sarcastic, and defended example of Chuckee. This persona morphs into the toxic Martyr archetype and I say, "Oh man, look at what I had to go through!" The Martyr quickly dissolves into a victim mindset/the Orphan archetype. This archetype voice says that no one will rescue me. My needs are too big, and I will always be alone.

My fear is not knowing how to get my needs met when I am in relationship with someone who is in their Orphan archetype and does not want to move out of that state, or someone whose pattern is familiar and entrenched and who is totally unaware of their expectations. This is a huge difficulty for me because I then get into my pattern of teaching so they can become aware (so familiar). Co-dependent behaviour at its finest! I once again tell myself, "If they would get it (become aware), I would be safe."

The learning for me is they do not need to get it. I need to "get it" that I can keep myself safe. I have come a long way in healing this codependency dynamic. The root of this is my parents and the schoolteacher who did not, would not get it.

As I shared previously, in many of my relationships, my needs were not acknowledged and of course not met. I believe my parents were not ever aware of my need for protection. The loud and clear message was "Do not need me" and "Need in silence." So, when someone close to me is not aware they are in their Orphan state and are unwilling to change, I project the messages I received as a child onto them. "Do not need me." "Need in silence."

I have difficulty serving a toxic Martyr/Orphan when I tell myself they expect me to serve them, they expect me to look after them, or that I must do so if I want to be in relationship and be safe. I do not want to give them anything. In fact, I can become quite mean (my defensive Chuckee manifesting) in order to back them off and not need me. (Same behaviour as my parents; do not need me). Of course, then comes the guilt and self-reproach. After they have backed off and I come out of beating myself up, then I can assess myself and figure out what it is I can give from my heart. I am very aware of where this pattern comes from, and I have healed much of the wound over the years. My question is, if I give to them, will I lose myself? How do I put a boundary in place and maintain it? How do I keep me safe or look after me? These are family of origin messages.

I realize I am in a double-bind situation. When I think I am needed by what I consider toxic person or someone who just expects me to meet their needs, I instantly become the teacher who says "No, I can't help you." If I say "Yes, I will help you," but then I don't, I am abandoning myself. Alas, and gratefully so, I am a work in progress.

I know the toxic Martyr in myself, the one who is fearful of being perceived as not getting it right or not being good enough. How I experience this archetype is quite paradoxical. I do not want to be needed or expected to be or do certain things; however, if you do not need me, then I am lost, and I gaslight or manipulate in some form so that I suck you back into needing me. In past circumstances, I needed to be externally validated to believe I had worth. Children all need external validation, and at some stage in development become their own validator. Missing this part of childhood development creates an ego need that can only be fulfilled from external sources until healing the trauma occurs.

I am also very aware of the Altruist/Martyr role in myself that is very pure and filled with love. I enjoy this part of the archetype. I have said for many years that God and I have a deal, an understanding; through Him, I do whatever work is in front of me, and He supplies everything else. This arrangement seems to work well.

I can get caught in the fear of how others will perceive my serving/ sacrifice. At times I have allowed my fear of rejection in this place to paralyze me, and therefore I abandon myself and what I know to be the right thing to do. Again, I call on the adult self or Big to step forward, take the journey, and act/do/be from the heart.

HOW DO FAITH AND GOD'S WORD INTERSECT WITH THE ALTRUIST/MARTYR ARCHETYPE? (KATHY)

"'But you were always a good man of business, Jacob,' faltered Scrooge, who now began to apply this to himself. 'Business!' cried the Ghost, wringing its hands again. 'Mankind was my business; charity, mercy, forbearance, and benevolence, were, all, my business. The deals of my trade were but a drop of water in the comprehensive ocean of my business!'"

—Charles Dickens, *A Christmas Carol*

It would seem the author Charles Dickens and the Bible would agree. Jesus says, "'Love the Lord your God with all your heart and with all your soul and with all your mind and with all your strength' . . . 'Love your neighbour as yourself.' There is no commandment greater than these" (Mark 12:30–31). It would seem mankind is indeed our business and love is the greatest commandment. The apostle Paul instructs us to ". . . Trust steadily in God, hope unswervingly, love extravagantly. And the best of the three is love." (*Message Bible*, 2018, 1 Corinthians 13:13). The altruist archetype is best illustrated through action with God's commandment to "love one another" (John 13:34).

As an Altruist, we accept the challenges and hardships of life and believe that as we journey these same obstacles and hardships have the potential to transform us. Jeremiah 18:5–6 uses the symbolism of transformation in the work of a potter: "Then the word of the Lord came to me. He said, 'Can I not do with you, Israel, as this potter does?' declares the Lord. 'Like clay in the hand of the potter, so are you in my hand, Israel.'" Just as the potter shapes the clay, I believe we are shaped by our experience and through our experience God will shape us into the person He created us to be. As the Altruist/Martyr archetype, our goal is to develop our gifts and abilities to nurture, help, or improve a situation by giving our time, our money, or our power. This is a fallen world. There are endless ways to sacrifice for others, for causes, for the world. The choices for the Altruist are almost limitless, ranging from extravagant acts of giving and sacrifice to the many and various altruist causes. Sharing what we have or giving of ourselves to the cause or causes that stir our heart and demand our attention helps us to find a sense of purpose and joy. The time to start can be now. There is no need to wait for perfection to begin to give of ourselves or to be rich to give money to the less fortunate or to have all our problems solved to help others solve problems.

The apostle Paul tells us in 2 Corinthians 12:8–9, "Three times I pleaded with the Lord to take it away from me. But he said to me, 'My grace is sufficient for you, for my power is made perfect in weakness.' Therefore, I will boast all the more gladly about my weaknesses, so that Christ's power may rest on me." The Bible encourages us to give as we can, any way we can, from our created soul. It is the act of giving that empowers us to stretch our soul and to become the person God has created us to be. As Altruists we can give whenever and whatever we have as we journey with others. After all, God not only commands us to love one another but to love His creation (Genesis 2:15) and its creatures (Genesis 1:26). It is our responsibility to care for others and our world whenever and however we can.

Sacrifice is a part of the Altruist/Martyr's journey and is a recurrent theme in the Bible. Examples of sacrifice are prevalent in the Old Testament. One way to think of sacrifice, animal, or harvest is that they were gifts form the Israelites to God. They gave of what they had to thank God for who He is and for their valued close relationship with Him. They were willing to sacrifice not only some of what they had but sometimes the best of what they had to deepen that relationship (the Book of Leviticus). The ultimate example of a sacrificial love story is found in the New Testament, God the Father's willingness to sacrifice His son Jesus (John 3:16, 17). Most of the references to sacrifice are in the Old Testament and although they seem complicated, upon study they are precursors, symbols, of the sacrifice of Christ on the cross. In the New Testament, almost all the references to sacrifice are predictions of that one prefect and complete sacrifice of Jesus: His payment for our sins.

The Webster's English Dictionary defines sacrifice as "to give up something that is valuable to you in order to help another person or the act of killing an animal or person and offering them to a god or gods, or the animal, etc. that is offered." After the ultimate sacrifice of the Lord Jesus in the New Testament, sacrifice is no longer necessary to live a life pleasing to God. However, the New Testament does refer to sacrifices we can willingly make in our daily lives that are pleasing to God, such as the sacrifice of worshiping God through praise (Hebrews 13:15), the living sacrifice of our bodies (Romans 12:1), and the sacrifice of doing good and sharing what we have (Hebrews 13:16). Finally, we sacrifice as a part of our love for others as defined in Romans 12:9–13:

> Love must be sincere. Hate what is evil; cling to what is good. Be devoted to one another in love. Honor one another above yourselves. Never be lacking in zeal, but keep your spiritual fervor, serving the Lord. Be joyful in hope, patient in affliction, faithful in prayer. Share with the Lord's people who are in need. Practice hospitality.

The ideology of the perfect Altruist is unachievable, so the logical fear of the Altruist becomes selfishness. This fear sometimes blurs the Altruist's boundaries from selflessness to being self-seeking or needing the reassurance that our altruistic good deeds are being recognized. This sometimes gives way to the shadow side of the altruist, the modern-day Martyr; someone that gives to receive something or so that everyone knows the depth of the sacrifice. The Bible tells us, "Be careful not to practice your righteousness in front of others to be seen by them. If you do, you will have no reward from your Father in heaven." (Matthew 6:1) The true Altruist's motive is love, not recognition. So, as the Altruist/Martyr archetype, we must learn to give from love, as well as to take care of ourselves and to heed the instruction of "love your neighbour as yourself".

The true Altruist acts from an internal motivation of love alone. If any number of other self-seeking, conflicting, external motives enter the journey of the Altruist archetype, the shadow side of the Altruist, the modern-day Martyr, as defined earlier in this chapter, is aroused. I believe we do not stray far from the Altruist archetype if we are able to internalize the Biblical definition of love found in Corinthians 13:5–7 (The Message, 2003):

Love never gives up.

Love cares more for others than for self.

Love doesn't want what it doesn't have.

Love doesn't strut,

Doesn't have a swelled head,

Doesn't force itself on others,

Isn't always "me first,"

Doesn't fly off the handle,

Doesn't keep score of the sins of others,

Doesn't revel when others grovel,

Takes pleasure in the flowering of truth,

Puts up with anything,

Trusts God always,

Always looks for the best,

Never looks back,

But keeps going to the end.

Kathy's Personal Experience of Scripture with the Altruist Archetype

I have been richly blessed! I treasure my God given life! Against the odds, here I am over twenty-five years cancer free! It hasn't always been easy. This journey has been full of potholes, hills, valleys, dark places of sadness, and places basking in the light of unexpected joy, and I don't deserve any of it. Every day is a gift!

The odds were not good as I battled with cancer. Though I believe and know in my heart that God is the ultimate physician, I also knew that as my part in the healing process I had to do everything possible to make life changes and healthy choices. So, my wandering began, and I drank Oriental fungus tea, studied, adhered to a healthy diet, learned about Creative Visualization techniques, prayed continually, chose to think positively, and agreed to undergo chemotherapy and radiation. I explored the mind, body, spirit connection, and I did everything I could think of doing to aid the healing process, but I left the entire outcome in God's hands, at least as much as humanly possible. Some of those days were dark, as I struggled with fear—the fear of death, fear of change, and fear of leaving my children behind. The day my oncologist said those most beautiful words, "You are in remission. For now, you are cancer free," I promised God that I would pour out my life for Him, and my conscious Altruist journey, began in earnest.

Placing one foot in front of the other on this journey is the easy part. The difficult part is to remember none of it is about me, it's all about God and the work I believe He has given me to do with the talents and gifts he has also given me (Ephesians 2:10). Sometimes the work seems to "appear", and I know it is for me to do, not just because I can do it and I have the skill to do it, but because God has prepared me to do it. At other times, I feel as if I'm knocking my head against the wall, searching for the right thing to do, but nothing seems right. I think that's when God is telling me to wait (Psalm 27:14). I'm not ready for the next challenge or the next bend in the road. This is a dangerous time because I know the toxic altruist is near. I lose confidence in myself and try to affirm my worth by seeking validation and reassurance from other people. The Orphan archetype is very close as I battle with my lack of self esteem and the fear of making a "mistake" or a bad choice. I fret over the way I think others are thinking of me or worry that other people are judging me. Some or none of this may be true, and this is the story that plays in my head until I can move on.

On the other hand, as I journey, God has from time to time given me the desires of my heart, sometimes, even before I knew how much they meant to me (Psalm 37:4). I was given the opportunity to edit a church newsletter with a talented and dedicated team of volunteers. I was given the opportunity to be the director of children's ministry, the leader of an awesome team of adult volunteers, and to be a member of the church board of directors. Through a God-directed path, I was able to achieve my dream of attending university to learn about teaching children in a church setting, and now I have the awesome opportunity to write this book with my good friend. I did not seek out any of these opportunities. It was as if God reached out His hand and gave me my heart's desire. As I did the work, struggled to manage the learning curve, and wrestled with the challenges and the opportunity itself, it was then that I realized not only was I working my dream, but this is also the work God has prepared for me to do. We are, however, imperfect humans, and as with all life experience, some of these opportunities (gifts) ended in heartache and in difficult life lessons, but God was with me in the journey, in the hurt, and in the learning (Matthew 28:20).

When working through my dreams and opportunities, I often need to remind myself, "It's not about me or anything I do. It's all about God's mercy and grace" (Ephesians 2:8-9) Nothing I can do will save me a place in heaven. It is a gift from God, bought through the death of Jesus on the cross. My desire to be more like Jesus must be my motivation for good works. Through God's leading, I attempt but often struggle to live God's two greatest commandments. Firstly, to love the Lord with all my heart and, secondly, to love my neighbour as myself (Luke 10:27). One of the most difficult situations I struggle with is recognition and praise. If I accept it for myself, I experience pride and then I'm sure to have a meltdown or a setback. If I don't, I struggle with graciously giving the recognition and praise to God without negating what some kind-hearted person has said to encourage and support me.

The other side of this same coin is struggling with no recognition. That's when I feel sorry for myself. I know when it's happening because I can hear my inner voice asking questions like, "Don't they know how long I worked on this project?" or "Don't they realize how tired I am or what I've sacrificed?" or "Why can't they give me a break or help out?" Then I know I've crossed the line. It's not about giving from my heart anymore. It's about giving to receive something in return. Again, the shadow Martyr is alive and well.

One of my favourite quotes is the one from Charles Dickens in *A Christmas Carol* found at the beginning of this section. I truly believe that "mankind is my business," and so the Altruist archetype is a recurrent theme in my life. However, I know that the true healthy Altruist must balance life with other archetypes to stay in tune with the created soul. For example, how can you help others if you don't recognize your Orphan archetype and learn what you need to be healthy and grow? How do you encourage others on the journey if you don't do your own wandering (Wanderer Archetype)? How can you fight for others if you do not fight for yourself (Warrior Archetype)? Life changes, and to stay in sync, we must change with it and learn to experience the changes as opportunities and gifts that challenge and help us to grow. It's always a struggle for me, but I know life is transformational (Romans 12:2), and I am so thankful that God is not finished with me yet (Philippians 1:6). Life is a gift, and with God's help, I can lead a life pleasing to him and make a difference one step at a time! I think this is the Altruist's hope and prayer.

SHARON'S PERSONAL EXPERIENCE OF SCRIPTURE WITH THE MARTYR ARCHETYPE

I was reminded a couple of days ago of a verse I used to hang onto, Ephesians 2:10: "God has created me anew in Christ Jesus to do the good works He has planned for me a long time ago." I know I have a path from God, and when I walk that path, which includes not being attached to things, my life is easy through His Grace. When I am not on that path, my experience is one of pushing the boulder up hill. I have a heavy, fear-filled feeling that all will crash down on me.

I have experienced others' Altruist archetype when I had no food and would take the kids for a drive and come home and a bag of groceries was on my steps. I have also done that same thing for others.

I have been characterized as strong-willed, headstrong, stubborn (I call it determined), willful. All true. God humbles me, and when I submit to His prodding, I am so richly blessed, and I get to see and experience His wonderful love for others. I know I do not need the resources to follow God. If I am walking/doing/being where and what He wants me to be, then He supplies all. He is faithful. My situation changes, I change, and God remains the same throughout the ages.

When I participate in giving or serving, I am reminded of the verse, "He [God] says when you do unto the least of these you have done also unto Me." (Matthew 25:40). For example, I loved my time developing and being involved in community breakfast. I gave all freely from my heart. Once I submitted to the God prod (only took two years), all the resources were available. No strings attached to or from anyone. What was given and received was pure service and caring.

Kathy and I were talking one day about our struggle with this archetype. I shared I had a difficult time accepting the Altruist/Martyr in myself in its intended manner. I remembered seeing a Joyce Meyers program where she discussed wearing a "do not disturb" sign around her neck, giving off an attitude that kept others away. Well, in the last few years, I have been wearing the "do not disturb" sign; I have not been paying attention to when God is providing an opportunity to serve.

As we were sharing, I got it; I understood my resistance. I could hear my mother saying, "Who do you think you are, Miss Mahatma Gandhi?" I was not supposed to do anything first or better than my brothers could or that she hadn't done or faced in her life. I learned to hide my light under a bushel. Yes, as Kathy points out, we are to give in secret, and I agree; however, we are not to hide out of fear. There is a place inside us that wants/needs to believe it is healthy to give and that it is God's will that we give and that He will bless us no matter what others in our world say. When service/giving is not instilled or praised or taught as a child, then the journey has another layer to heal that of shame. Giving and serving has become entwined with duty, hence the shame and guilt when the image of the Altruist is not lived up to. This is internalizing external values and beliefs, creating either pride or shame when we do not measure up.

I am grateful that (loosely paraphrased) He tells us that once He has started a work in us, He is faithful to complete it (Philippians 1:6). Work in progress—that will be the sign I now carry around my neck.

CHAPTER THREE
The Wanderer
(Sharon)

T HE WANDERER ARCHETYPE provides opportunities to explore boundaries and barriers to embarking on the healing journey.

The goal of the Wanderer: To discover the true self, or a gift that represents the true self; to identify the "Dragon" and escape. The Dragon refers to any obstacle or barrier that creates fear and impedes our journey. The book *Face the Fear and Do It Anyway* (1987) by author Susan Jeffers comes to mind. It shares ideas of finding courage to overcome fears. Whether the journey be internal or external, there is always a searching, a breaking away from the old, which will involve living in liminal spaces for a while. One would definitely not be in the Orphan archetype.

Goal of abandonment: To self-regulate, break patterns. Face the fear and move forward; move out of your comfort zone. Learning how to self-soothe. Become all you can be even if there is fear. This way of being allows you to be your authentic self or true self, not motivated by fear. You would be the adult part of yourself operating from the prefrontal cortex, or "Big."

The next archetype, the Wanderer, involves the journey of growth. I believe discovering the self by taking our own distinct, separate journey is a life-long endeavour. The Wanderer archetype invites us to go into the very depths of ourselves and stir up the muck, and get dirty to find and change the patterns we have developed (behaviourally, and the neuropathways in our brains) over the years so we may live in the world around us in a healthy way, not conforming to societal expectations but growing and transforming so we may in turn be transformers. This desire for growth and change, to push and achieve is in opposition to the desire to fit in and please (codependency). To embark on this journey means breaking free of the captivity state of the Orphan. Living in the journey of the Wanderer archetype, we respond rather than react.

We learn how to survive as the Orphan by hiding or putting parts of ourselves away. We exiled the parts of us deemed unacceptable to others or to ourselves, probably at a young age. Perhaps we were shamed for these parts or rejected in some manner for certain aspect of ourselves. We thus learned to hide them in a bid for emotional safety. This is a learned coping defense mechanism.

As I mentioned previously, I was shamed for being smart or intelligent, so I hid that part of myself. The Wanderer archetype bids us to move from the Orphan into the realm of the unknown to find the self or the parts we put away a long time ago in order to survive. The Wanderer's journey is to find and be the self we are meant to be in every situation we experience, to explore and show those hidden parts of ourselves, and to identify the barriers we erected to keep us from embarking on the journey of self-discovery.

Each experience lived fully ages us like fine wine. The Wanderer archetype, in contrast to Orphan and Innocent, requires us to become conscious—conscious of ourselves and the world around us. It is in this archetype we step up and become responsible for our lives, the choices, decisions, the consequences, all of it. We are responsible. It is our life. Sometimes we are too fearful to take our journey, to break away and become separate. Instead of taking our journey, we may learn to hide by playing roles, by wearing masks, by isolating and by being the Orphan or the toxic Martyr by defending, or the toxic side of Warrior, which is another manifestation of Chuckee.

It is my experience that when our family of origin background involves scarcity of the basic needs, as well as emotional scarcity, we bring that fear with us into our adult world. My Pastor calls it living in Scare City. I think we have a belief and fear that what we really need is in short supply and that we better hang onto what we have. This creates another layer of challenges to overcome when we take the Wanderer's journey. Exploring, finding, and changing belief systems we had put in place when we were very young is part of the journey. If we have a belief system, from our family of origin, that says "there is never enough," most times we internalize this as "I am not enough." The Wanderer's journey confronts our trust issues with both self and others. I have learned to trust that I am my best resource and that I can keep me safe.

Perhaps some questions can assist you in exploring those belief systems. What is it you really want/desire in your life? What stops you? Where did that pattern, those beliefs, come from? Do you want to hold on to them? Do they assist you in attaining your goals or do they impede you? Where is your creative side? When you were young, eight and nine years old, what excited you in terms of "I want to do that when I grow up?" This is the time to engage the creative side of you, the imaginative part. Self-reflection is one of the tools we can use to become conscious, break up the old mental set, make a change, and step into the unknown. We venture into liminal space—no longer in the old, and the new is not there yet.

One way to discover what your Wanderer journey might be is to recall a dream or a longing deep in your soul, your heart. The words may be something like, "I wish I could . . ." or "When I was nine, I wanted . . ." The ending to those wishes and dreams is usually, "But I can't because I have obligations, what if someone is upset, or who will do…?" Usually when we use the word "but," the comment is coming from a Chuckee state (a defended state), a state of fear and defensiveness that will keep the patterns the same. The above-mentioned fears and obligations may be real, or we may use them to prevent us from creating and facing uncomfortable change. The role of this voice or state is to keep you safe or to protect you; however, it is an illusion of safety as you remain in the same state, a state of familiarity. We can often confuse familiarity with safety. The question then becomes, "Am I safe or have I only returned to a state of familiar patterns to reduce my tension?"

Our journey does not have to be grand or big. It does, however, move us through fear, fear of either doing, saying, or being in some manner, which is fraught with potential risk. The risk is either emotional, financial, physical, mental, or spiritual and emerges whether these fears are real or perceived as real. These are all the Dragons (fears) you shied away from when you were not safe to make change. Perhaps the situations you were in when you were younger were unsafe, and you did have to fit in or please or modify yourself to survive. The journey now that you are no longer that child is to distinguish between then and now, and to realize that you do not need to hold onto patterns from those situations.

A journey can look like asking for a raise when you have never in your life acted on this type of thought, or perhaps buying a new home, thus thwarting the notion you are selfish, or a new used home is good enough. Your journey may be to travel by yourself. It may begin with being part of a tour and graduate to holidays for one. I have watched people bask in the freedom of facing the fear of going to dinner alone (without a book) or going to the movies alone or writing a book, no matter how long it takes. These actions assist in discovering the answer to the question, "Who am I when I face the fear of self rejection and step out?" "Who am I when I choose not to reject myself any longer?" My granddaughter says, "I took myself on a date last night". How wonderful that sounds to me.

Stepping out of your comfort zone and reflecting allows you an opportunity to become even more aware of who and where you are in your life, and you can begin to explore how you may have been creating pieces of your journey in experiences that you have already encountered or created. For example, perhaps you have always wanted to go to university and get a degree, something that is outside the norm of your family's expectations. You might want to look at the books on your shelf; are they connected in any way to your dream of university? Have you ever taken an online course? Have you taken any college/university courses? Have you upgraded? All of these are ways you are preparing yourself to break free. These experiences, when seen from this perspective, help us create the Lifting stage in abandonment. The Lifting stage is where we have hope. We experience a lightness that says there is a light at the end of the tunnel.

As you explore your left-behind dreams, you may become aware of some resentment or anger. This suppressed anger/resentment also suppresses our creative side. The energy created by the feeling of anger can be used to assist in making plans to resurrect some of those dreams in some manner. I believe finding those dreams and plans can assist you in doing the soul work so necessary in finding those parts of yourself that you lost/pushed down, rejected, or exiled.

In an ever-changing world, I think it is important that we all take our journey so we can take our place and in turn raise children, either our own or as a role model for others' children. These children can then take their place in the world and be part of community making a difference. This journey demands we step into our adult role and move forward. Each step we take is significant as we heal from the wounds of abandonment.

Abandonment in the Wanderer Archetype

Abandonment can be experienced by the Wanderer in differing ways; You may be abandoned by others or by yourself. Again, let us use the SWIRL format to explore these ways.

SWIRL

Shattering

Shattering is experienced in the Wanderer archetype when we decide to take our journey. We shatter our way out of the Orphan by coming out of denial and out of being the toxic Martyr by believing that we are enough, we have inherent worth, and our needs are valid. This means breaking the old familiar patterns of how we get those needs met. When patterns begin to break/change, Little becomes quite fearful, firstly because Little is afraid of change, and secondly because we are afraid of others' rejection. We may hear our own voice saying, "Oh, I can't believe I quit my job! I can't believe I am moving! I can't believe I broke up my relationship!" We become aware of a tightening someplace in our bodies which signals to the brain that there is impending danger. The brain reacts with the flooding of adrenaline ready to defend. Calming and regulating ourselves is key, or else Chuckee will be alive and well in our world, maintaining all the old patterns, preventing us from taking our journey, keeping us in the same familiar patterns.

Chuckee is the great saboteur. This voice can be quite seductive in convincing you that what you want to do can wait or perhaps something better will come along. We also are fearful of ourselves, not quite trusting that we will follow through or even make choices that are in our best interests. We need to build a trust history with ourselves to help assuage the doubts and fears of Little. We need to capture all our successes, all our changes and make them conscious. In doing so, we break up the old familiar mental sets and create new neurological pathways.

Part of Shattering is something called split-thinking (Anderson). In common language, it is spoken of as the glass being half empty, the perspective that we need a whole loaf, not half a loaf. It is the all-or-nothing mindset. This mindset does not allow acknowledgement of incremental achievements in our pursuit of autonomy. This belief keeps us in a place of thinking "if it can't be this or it can't be that, then it can't be anything." I think in split-thinking we can easily end up in the powerlessness of the Orphan archetype.

Embracing the notion that it is healthy to be intimate/connected/attuned and yet remain separate because we are separate people with our own personalities is an important aspect of learning how to be in relationship. Rather than being codependent, we become interdependent. The messages we may give ourselves at this time are from the mindset of scarcity—scarcity of love. We tell ourselves we are much better off holding on to what we already have because there may not be anyone else who will love us, saying, "After all I am fat, old, wrinkly," or whatever we may tell ourselves. The fear of being intimate (not sexual) is at times almost palpable.

Janet Woititz (1985), in *Struggle for Intimacy*, talks about distancer and pursuer roles as both involving the fear of intimacy. The belief embedded in these roles is "If I let you get too close, you will suffocate me, and if I am not stuck to you like a Velcro strip, you will forget and abandon me." In this dynamic, there isn't any individuation or separateness. Lack of boundaries and self-worth, help to create this dynamic. These are old beliefs, barriers (Dragons) that we change a step at a time in the Wanderer journey. Learning how to be alone/separate and become your own "best resource" is so essential to integrating all the parts of us and to breaking the old familiar patterns and stepping out onto a new journey.

Withdrawal

In the withdrawal stage of abandonment when we are taking our journey in the Wanderer archetype, we may experience isolation and loneliness, and we may wish for a return to the familiar past and patterns. This is Little wanting to be attached. Big does not want to return; however, the pull and longing to be attached can be very strong. When the adult perseveres, they meet others travelling the same less travelled road. These new relationships will be healthier.

We may experience a body sensation that is akin to wanting to crawl out of our skin, feeling agitated, and having an intense amount of frustration (Anderson). All these sensations and feelings can lead to thinking perhaps we made a mistake, or we need to "fix" things (relieve the inner tension) by returning to the previous situation. We go into self-doubt, which is definitely a huge clue that Chuckee is sabotaging.

Breaking patterns and facing fears automatically changes relationships. When relationships change, there is a potential for loss, and when we are not in a relationship, the adrenaline level drops. Adrenaline is addictive. The body experiences we are having, as mentioned in the previous paragraph, are withdrawal from the higher level of adrenaline. When we return to familiar patterns, or even think about returning, there is an ease for a short amount of time because we did get a "fix" because the adrenaline was raised. Then Big emerges (our thinking returning to the frontal lobe from the amygdala), and we are so upset with ourselves because we are doing same old, same old yet again.

We gradually learn to be more compassionate with ourselves as we continue the journey. Going back is not "bad"; it is a part of the journey. We are making new neuropathways in our brain. When we break out of the old patterns and form new neuropathways, we no longer attract or are attracted to the same people or activities that once attracted us. We usually get "change back" messages from friends and family. When we break away and change relationships, those we left behind experience loss and a fear of being abandoned. If they are wounded and have not done the work of healing, their Chuckee is activated, and they act out in some manner. They could become the Orphan or the toxic Martyr in order to help soothe their Little's feelings of loss.

Internalizing the Rejection

Some of those "change back" messages mentioned above include "I really miss how we used to be," or "How can you leave a good paying job like that?" or "Wow, your parents are aging, what will they do without you?" Sometimes we take that on, which means we internalize the messages and tell ourselves that perhaps they are right. We think, "I am selfish. I do need that job. How can I do this to people."

This fear is coming from Little. The actions when we return to the familiar are Chuckee. Remember, Chuckee's job is to keep all the patterns the same and to protect Little from feeling afraid. This voice of condemnation is very old. We learned these messages at an early age, and now it is time to refute those messages before we act on them in a Chuckee manner, which is how we do to ourselves what has been done to us and keep ourselves stuck in captivity in the Orphan state. It is time to find your own truth and act from that position.

Rage

I like this stage of abandonment. I am going to use "I" language for some of this section. This is the stage where I take back my power and make a plan that will assist me in moving forward on my journey. I refute the lies, begin to believe in myself, listen to myself, and not take on other's opinions of what is right for my life. Often in the beginning, the only way I can stand in for myself is through a storm of rage. I learn as I go how to be calmer and more assertive; however, in the beginning, my voice and words can be less than pretty.

I take others off the pedestal of authority, take myself out of the ditch, and stop abandoning myself. This stage can also be very toxic and hurtful as we negotiate loss or the fear of rejection. This toxic place can look like blame which can be the Orphan or the Martyr. My voice may be crying out, saying, "Fix it, you broke it!"

Or I may lash out as the toxic part of Warrior (which shall be discussed further in the next chapter). For example, I may think that if I speak softly, my words and being will not be respected or that I will dissolve the new boundaries for which I fought so hard. After the railing and lashing against reality, I beat myself up for my actions and then return to withdrawal, internalization, and the Orphan, thinking, "Perhaps I made a mistake. I can't do this. I need to fix it." This is a Chuckee sabotage message creating self-doubt and keeping patterns the same. The Wanderer can identify the Dragons, the barriers, and not always be able to circumvent them. Creating and maintaining boundaries can be challenging, and we do not always act in a healthy manner.

In this state, I need to become the adult part of me or call on the healthy part of the Warrior and continue in my journey with all my feelings, including fear, intact, without spiritually bypassing or lifting out of and over the feelings.

Lifting

We can experience lifting even before we have decided in the rage stage to break away by allowing ourselves to have our dream, by daydreaming about it, by speaking about it with safe people, by becoming conscious, catching a glimpse of the ways we can have some of our dream right now. We then experience a sense of relief, an inner peace, a calming, a sense of light at the end of the tunnel. HOPE. Even if this stage is intermittent and brief, you still have it within you as a template, and you can recreate that feeling whenever you choose.

How Do Faith and God's Word Intersect With the Wanderer Archetype? (Kathy)

"For I know the plans I have for you, declares the
Lord, plans to prosper you and not to harm you,
plans to give you hope and a future."
—Jeremiah 29:11

Have you ever felt trapped? Have you ever asked yourself, "Is this all there is to life?" I believe that is the call of the Wanderer. It is the archetype that begins to realize that life is not all suffering, but it is an endless adventure!

As an Innocent, we must in due time experience the fall from paradise to grow. As an Orphan, we seek safety and learn to find trust and hope in a fallen world. As a Wanderer, we search for identity; we set out on a quest to find ourselves. When we refuse to be the person others want us to be and choose to discover who God created us to be and, therefore, meant us to be, we discover the Wanderer within us.

With the Wanderer archetype comes a curious mix of emotions. These feelings include fear of upsetting or alienating others and fear that our loved ones may not love us anymore if we are not who we seem to be. We may feel uncertainty, the feeling that the rug has been pulled from beneath us as we move away from familiar patterns and sometimes familiar relationships. However, we also feel excited to experience and learn what is just around the corner and contentment and joy when we find our unique self, our soul, and we can reach out to others as our true selves. Though there may be uncertainty and fear, "Trust in the Lord with all your heart and lean not on your own understanding; in all your ways acknowledge him, and he will make your paths straight" (Proverbs 3:5–6).

Often, we find our faith, our spirituality, as a Wanderer. When our lives do not seem to work or make sense anymore, we do not feel satisfied. Sometimes we feel trapped by circumstances and/or the expectations of other people, often the very people that love us the most. Intuitively, we know that we must escape, rise above our situations, and become the person we were meant to be, not only the sum part of our circumstances and what others expect of us. Sometimes we think we do not belong in our current place; we do not feel comfortable in our own skin anymore, and so we search to find significant meaning and the depth of and security of believing in something more than ourselves. This is the point where some reach out to a Greater Good, or for me, God. When we seek in that manner, we find God waiting:

> Ask and it will be given to you; seek and you will find; knock and the door will be opened to you. For everyone who asks receives; the one who seeks finds; and to the one who knocks, the door will be opened. (Matthew 7:7–8)

The Bible is full of stories about wandering (Genesis 3:6; Numbers 32:13; 1 Peter 2:12). The most well-known story is about Moses and the Israelites wandering in the desert for forty years following God to the Promised Land in the book of Exodus. In this story, the Israelites were wandering with God to God's Promised Land. However, the Wanderer archetype in the Bible is, also depicted as wandering away from God and the path of righteousness: "We all, like sheep, have gone astray, each of us has turned to our own way; and the Lord has laid on him the iniquity of us all" (Isaiah 53:6).

God's Word tells us many times in both the Old and New Testaments that we are always welcome to return to Him after our wanderings. Jeremiah 24:7 promises a way back to God when it says, "I will give them a heart to know me, that I am the Lord. They will be my people, and I will be their God, for they will return to me with all their heart." I believe taking our personal journey is essential to discover our authentic self, which is the person we were created to be, and our true beliefs.

When we are honest with ourselves and turn to look back at our lives, we know that we have not always done everything well or "right." It is a mark of our humanity that we make mistakes and sometimes make decisions that hurt others. Guilt and shame are part of the human condition, but we do not have to carry them: "For all have sinned and come short of the glory of God" (Romans 3:23). God made us uniquely in His own image (Isaiah 64:8). He knew we would make mistakes, unwise and unhealthy choices, but He loves us, and ". . . God demonstrates His own love toward us, in that while we were still sinners, Christ died for us" (Romans 5:8) Jesus Christ died for you and for me so that we have a way to be with God forever (Romans 6:23). There is a way for us to leave our mistakes behind, to be forgiven (1 John 1:9). God gives us a way to anchor our wanderings and belong to something much bigger than ourselves, the kingdom of God (Romans 10:9). We are free to live in the unique way God created for us, free to take our journeys and free to do the work God created for us to do (Ephesians 2:10). We are secure in God's promise. "I am convinced that neither death nor life, neither angels or demons, neither the present not the future, nor any powers, neither height nor depth, nor anything else in all creation, will be able to separate us from the love of God that is in Jesus Christ our Lord." (Romans 8:38-39). It is through the love of God that we can experience life anew every morning (Lamentations 3:22-23).

Though I believe that wandering to find our spiritual belief system, whatever that turns out to be, is fundamental to the journey of the Wanderer, there are other ways the Wanderer archetype enters our lives. Whenever we determine to change our circumstances (work, relationships, living situation, etc.), we take on the Wanderer archetype with all its risks and uncertainties and potential joy and contentment. We set out to find the Promised Land, the place where life is rich, and we can be authentic.

The key for me in my life's journey is to follow the plan, the path God has prepared for me (Jeremiah 29:11, the verse that opens this section). I journey to find the work God created for me to do (Ephesians 2:10) with the spiritual gifts (1 Corinthians 12:28) and natural talents He gave me (1 Corinthians 12:5–6) as I strive to treat others the way I would like to be treated (Mark 12:31).

During my life's journey, I can be assured and secure in the knowledge that when I stray or wander away, God still loves me, and He will welcome me back just like the father in the story of the Prodigal Son welcomed back his son. In this story, the youngest son had taken on the Wanderer archetype and gone off with his portion of his inheritance to seek his fortune apart from his father and older brother. When his plans went awry, and he found himself in a desperate situation he went home. His father welcomed him with open arms, but his older brother was not as forgiving and did not understand why his father would be so generous to the younger brother after his selfish and neglectful behaviour. However, the father said, ". . . we had to celebrate and be glad, because this brother of yours was dead and is alive again; he was lost and is found" (Luke 15:31). What a peaceful and loving picture of God's opened arms!

KATHY'S PERSONAL EXPERIENCE WITH THE WANDERER ARCHETYPE

As the Wanderer, I faced a very frightening time simultaneously with a period of significant personal growth when I was diagnosed with cancer. There was a long string of incidents that I attribute to God's guidance leading me to the place of diagnosis. The story begins just after I was married the second time (my first marriage is another story). My new husband was a teacher from Manitoba. He enjoyed life to the fullest and encouraged me to live my life differently. I found myself laughing more and experiencing not just the responsibilities and struggles of life, but the fun and joy of living! I felt accepted for who I am and free to be me.

Life was not totally carefree, though. I was working for the bank, not quite full time, thirty-two hours a week, and he was having trouble finding a teaching position in British Columbia. His teaching certificate was from Manitoba, and without significant upgrading, teaching in British Columbia was not an option. We were raising two school-age children together, so money was tight for both of us. After we married, we decided to leave Victoria and head to the Yukon Territories so that my husband could accept a position with the Yukon Government teaching "at risk" Children.

Just before we embarked on our move, I began having trouble with my left eye. The focus was off, I saw star bursts, and the lid seemed to be swollen. I went to see the doctor, and he said that he thought it was caused from allergies but couldn't be sure. Unfortunately, he said, we were going in the wrong direction for testing; medical facilities were few and far between in the North, so I should watch it and seek medical treatment if it did not improve or became worse.

I loved the Yukon; the sights, the sounds, the smells, the feeling of living in the North, and the need to be self-sufficient! I loved hiking above the tree line and watching for grizzly bears. I was thrilled to see the gigantic sun peaking over the horizon on the shortest day. The sight of an almost perfect circle of Northern Lights crackling and dancing over our heads in the dead of night is etched in my memory forever. Life was good! We were happy as a couple and happy as a family. I was too busy to bother about my eye or even give it a second thought.

One Sunday morning, as I was preparing to teach Sunday school, I turned my head to the side and looked in the mirror. I was startled, aghast, to see a white lump on the left side of my left eye. Now that I had seen it, when I looked straight ahead, I could see the skin tightly covering a swelling. It was neither a soft lump nor a hard lump. It felt like flesh, but I knew it did not belong. I told myself it was a swelling due to allergies, but decided to go to the clinic to check it out because though no doctor was attached to the clinic, a nurse was always on duty. My blood pressure was sky high; the nurse said it was in the stroke-producing range. The nearest hospital for testing was about 250 miles away, and she couldn't think of another reason for the swelling in my eyelid, so decided it must be an allergic reaction. Unable to prescribe medicine for high blood pressure, she sent me home with allergy drops and instructions to watch my diet and rest.

This is where God intervened. Very suddenly, my husband's position with the Yukon government was terminated. We were on our way home to BC in the dead of winter! I was immediately thrust into the middle of a very difficult move with a distraught husband and two school-age children. With God's help and strength, we made it back to Vancouver Island, back to the security of family and friends. My husband soon found a new position with social services helping and supporting children in the system. I was too busy to think about me. I was encouraging my husband as much as possible, easing my children back into new schools in a new school district, and desperately trying to help and support my mom, who was struggling with leukemia. When I was finally able to stop and take a breath, I realized that I was not well! I was tired all the time. The swelling in my eye was no worse but no better and my sight seemed to be getting worse. Reading had become a challenge.

The diagnostic process was slow but the usual sequence: family doctor, eye specialist, ocular oncologist, and then the testing process with needles in the eye and sitting still endlessly while intravenous solutions ran through my system. When I was able to process my situation, I realized this "stuff" running through my blood system was poison, and I was angry—at God, at myself, at the universe at large. It was determined by an ocular oncologist in Vancouver that the lump was a lymphoid tumour (cancer) encased in the conjunctive sack. An operation was scheduled immediately. The surgery was a success, and they said they got it all. However, I think I knew intuitively that the cancer was not gone. Looking in the mirror, just after the swelling from surgery had dissipated; I saw a horrifying pink row of "flesh" just above the bottom lid. The doctor said it was okay, but somewhere inside I knew it was not okay.

Those are the facts, but during this time, my Wanderer was awakened. I was angry at the cancer and tired of looking after everyone else, caring for their needs and not my own. I was striving to be the best person I could be, the best wife, mother, daughter, sister. I was running so fast and trying so hard to meet the expectations of other people that I forgot about taking care of me, meeting my own expectations. There was no joy or wonder in my life anymore. I was acutely aware that life is short on this Earth, yet when I searched my soul, I had no answers to fundamental questions. Who was I? What did I want from life? What did I believe?

I began to question my life, my beliefs, my God. I searched scripture for answers to my questions. I studied Buddhism, even though I was fearful that studying another religion might be insulting to the Christian God. I was compelled to learn and grow. I journaled and I read everything I could lay my hands on concerning the body, mind, and soul connection. Bernie Siegal, author of *Love, Medicine and Miracles* (1986) became my favourite author. Through his books, I learned about the essence of hope, the value of not being a statistic but rather a story, and the practice of counting my blessings.

I didn't know then, but God was preparing me and allowing me to struggle as the Wanderer archetype to discover some of life's truths and begin my conscious journey to fight a life-threatening and life-altering battle later, a story that will be further explored when we discuss the Warrior archetype.

SHARON'S PERSONAL EXPERIENCE WITH THE WANDERER ARCHETYPE

To date, my journey would include writing this book. I cannot talk about the material and not do it, "it" referring to the work of exploring and healing whatever comes to the surface as I read and write. The work is facing my fears and embracing all the concepts I am writing about. The journey of co-writing is very new and again affords me the opportunity to experience stretch marks on the psyche. My children used to become so upset when I would say, "Oh, another golden O." I think if memory serves me correctly that saying comes from Louise Hay.

I was the one in group projects at school who had the vision and then watched the group scramble and stumble and then come to the same vision. I would wait—sometimes patiently, sometimes not—until they came to the same resolution. I had the original visionary idea of the book. Now Kathy and I are visionary partners in carrying out the process and birthing the book. My roles traditionally have been one up or one down from the Wanderer, Orphan, or Warrior. Now we are Wanderers together and I embrace the opportunity to learn, grow and change. Am I fearful? Yes. Am I still going to continue the journey? For sure.

Coming from a family, where it seemed there wasn't any room for me, I was always unconsciously invoking the Wanderer archetype and wanting to get away. I remember when my friend and I were about eleven, we would walk about a half hour to the next little community and walk up and down the streets looking at places where we imagined and dreamed, we could live. Her home life was not so wonderful either. I would say things like, "There's a garage big enough to make into a one room apartment." Ironically, every home I have owned, except the one I am now in, has had a garage, and the first thing I did after purchase was to renovate the garage into a suite. I laughed when I became aware of the pattern and how I was playing out that childhood need to always ensure I had a room.

When I was twelve, I went to another province to live with relatives. When I returned a year later, nothing had changed so I packed a suitcase and left. I walked out in the middle of the afternoon in front of everyone and no one said anything. I couch surfed before that was even a popular thing for teens to do. I always went to school and had one or two jobs as well as a host of awesome amazing friends, some of whom I am still in contact with.

At seventeen years of age, I became pregnant, and in 1967 gave birth to my son, at age eighteen whom I placed for adoption. We have reunited. That was a very big Wanderer path of unconsciously breaking familiar patterns. I am not sure I even have words to describe this time in my life except heartbreak, betrayal, and gut-wrenching aloneness. Again, the female authority figures of social workers both for Children's Aid Society and for the hospital betrayed and did not protect me.

When I married in the 70s, I think I knew I was marrying for the wrong reason. The Little part of me wanted to be attached and taken care of. The Orphan wanted to be taken care of, and Chuckee said "I do!" It turned out that he needed more taking care of than I did and needed more than I was willing to or knew how to give. We went back and forth over seven years and two daughters, finally separating for good when the children were three and five. Being a single parent in the 70s held a very definite stigma, being viewed as something unhealthy. Single mothers were looked down upon and ostracized. I struggled financially, working as a licensed practical nurse. Many babysitters were hired, fired, and quit. I faced struggle after struggle with family only a few blocks away. Leaving a marriage was taboo in our family. My mother's motto was "you made your bed; you lie in it." Once again, the Wanderer inside me identified and broke barriers embedded in societal norms and survived.

I have so many Wanderer stories, as I imagine we all have. The above are just a few examples. I think I live in this state much of the time, healing, learning, growing. For as long as I can remember, I have had this desire, this yearning to live remote, off the land, secluded in an area where I could experience all the seasons. Hmmm, is this an unconscious need to manifest the three-year-old on the snow drift with God? I wonder. I want the knowledge that I could do it, that I could reach some "end" of me. I guess that could be called reaching potential in the area of survival or resourcefulness and proving that I was capable.

I also wonder if this is a repeat pattern of believing I cannot trust anyone except myself. My growing-up years were filled with messages of my stupidness, my never amounting to anything, my never reaching potential, and my lack of capability. Perhaps this dream or longing was to face the fears that maybe they were right, that all those messages might have been accurate. My journey was very fear-filled because, as much as I longed to live in this secluded, natural place, I would find many things to prevent me from taking the necessary steps to do so. Chuckee would sabotage because while I did not want the people in my past to be right, I was afraid taking the journey would prove they were right. So, Chuckee would say things like, "Many people depend on you," "You are not secure financially," convincing me to stay put.

The other message I received that fit in with my pattern of never taking my Wanderer's journey was that I was so inept I needed people. For years I played these mixed messages over and over in my head. "Don't need anyone because if you do, that will prove you can't do anything on your own!" What an Orphan/Little place.

One day, I began to realize that situations I had been experiencing and creating were actually part of the journey dream. I bought a fairly remote property home and slowly made plans to landscape. I brought in gravel, bought sturdy shovels, and began making a gravelled pathway around the perimeter of the property. I found this work immensely satisfying and soul nourishing. I sectioned off a piece for a garden, dug post holes, and put up a fence to keep critters out. I loved it, and one day when I was having lunch with a friend who was a real estate agent, much to my surprise, I asked her if she had time to come out and list my house. I had never before had a thought in my head about selling. I guess I had come to the end of that journey.

I created many aspects of my long-dreamed journey in this experience. I faced many of the self-imposed blocks (what if someone sees me in the yard? or what if I make a mess?) during the time on this property. Financially, I lost my job four months after purchase. The purchase of this property and the ability to maintain it is a God story for sure, perhaps to share in another book. I have since created more of the journey without the full experience. I am aware now how I tell myself messages like, "I am too old, my health isn't what it used to be, I don't want to worry my kids." These messages keep me stuck in the place I am in. I do look for ways I can create more of my journey, asking if I can rent a place in an area that experiences seasonal changes, if I can I tour a remote place, and how else I can take this journey. Now, I do intentionally go to dinner alone and sit isolated without watching others. Taking my Wanderer's journey looks different than I believed I needed it to look.

Today, when I am looking for property in the remote hills of Scotland, I know I have abandoned myself and that Chuckee is running away, which is not the Wanderer's journey. The Wanderer's journey is to remain and heal my relationships, although in some respects, it is easier, I think, sometimes to be isolated.

I realize that although I am living in very close proximity to people, I have a road that is in the woods, and I do not walk there. I can feel the fear of not being safe. What if, what if? Some of the fears are legitimate. I also know I can circumvent those legitimate fears and I have not done so. I need to summon help from one of the other Archetypes and remain in the adult part of me, aware, conscious, and intentional. Anytime I am identifying Dragons and changing patterns I am returning to the Wanderer archetype.

SHARON'S PERSONAL EXPERIENCE OF SCRIPTURE WITH THE WANDERER ARCHETYPE

"Lean not on your own understanding. In all thy ways
acknowledge Him and He shall direct your path."
—Proverbs 3: 5–6

"I will instruct you and teach you in the way you should
go. I will counsel you with my loving eye upon you."
—Psalm 32:8

"Your word is a lamp to my feet and a light to my path."
—Psalm 199:105

No matter where I journeyed, either emotionally or spiritually, I always knew God was beside me. From the three-year-old sitting on the snowbank to the me at the age I am today, He is always there. The passages of scripture that Kathy shared are dear to me, and I have claimed them and rested in them daily. I believe I am here because God has a plan for me. I do not know His plan, only that He does have one. The awesome thing is, I do not need to know what the plan is. If I knew, I would be "helping" God, AKA getting in His way. I think of the lines in the verse in my song, "One Set of Footprints" where I speak of wandering through the years, masking all my fears, looking for answers from everyone I met. I know now that my answers and my way home were always found in God.

When I am on God's path for my life, I experience an ease, a peace, a lightness. That is God's grace, which is sufficient unto me. When I have a plan, or I want something to happen, I experience a struggle, a frustration, setbacks, and a headache from banging my head against a door God has closed. There isn't any room for God's grace when I do that. God may give me some of what I want or even allow my plan to go ahead at times. He also allows me to have consequences.

In my wanderings, I have trod down paths other Christians informed me there was no coming back from. They told me those paths would get me thrown into the lake of fire and it was probably too late to save me. These "friends" (brothers and sisters in Christ) rejected me and ostracized me in the church. I was afraid, and I was also angry because I knew God was right at my side allowing me to carry on. Christian people would shun me, push me out, and even when I struggled to feed my children and they were aware of this, they didn't provide any help (a familiar betrayal). The message I internalized was, "If you could just be a better Christian, God would be blessing you, and you wouldn't be having these problems." That view of God is so different than the God I believed in. I was hurt and angry and confused and left the church. I left the church, not God, and God did not leave me. He was and is consistent and constant.

When I reached the end of my plan for my life and surrendered, God was very quick to completely restore me to Himself (Jeremiah 29). In fact, He gave back all the years the locusts ate, as He promised in scripture. The prodigal returned home.

One of the scriptures I hang onto in my Wanderer's journey is when Jesus in Luke 17:14 tells the lepers as they go, they will be healed. He didn't say "Wait here; you will be healed," He said go. So, as I go, I will be healed. To me this means as I take my journey guided by Him and face my fears and become who He created me to be in the first place, I am being healed in each step.

I wrote two songs about fifteen years ago titled "I'll Take The Next Step" and "I Seek You Lord." These songs speak of a journey finding God, finding my identity in God, and trusting God. Learning to fully trust is such a huge journey for me, as I am challenged to surrender, explore, examine, and release the fear and hurt from family, school, the church, and friends. The journey to learn how to trust fully so that I can be safe in each moment, is still a work in progress.

"For He will command his angels concerning you to guard you in all your ways;" (Psalm 91 11).

CHAPTER FOUR

The Warrior
(Sharon)

THE ROLE OF the Warrior Archetype is to learn how to manage the Dragons identified by the Wanderer Archetype. The Warrior learns how to surrender and give in, not give up, and to allow the self to become. This is a part of the journey where there is a letting go of the struggle and fight. The Warrior makes a clear pathway to follow as we navigate SWIRL and scripture.

Goal of the Warrior archetype: To slay the Dragon the Wanderer identified and then fled. To stand up for self. To rescue self.

Goal of Abandonment: To learn how to stand up to fear. Live from the frontal lobe/adult regulated state; to respond rather than react.

An important question for this archetype is "Who is the Dragon?"

The message given to the Orphan from the Warrior is one of rescue and care. When we are first beginning our Warrior journey, we are moving from a position of the Orphan, who is seeking a rescuer, and the Wanderer, who is journeying to discover the self, and learning the names of the Dragons, (internal or external obstacles or opponents), that block the journey. The Warrior's journey is to confront and slay the Dragons, whether these Dragons be physical, mental, emotional, or spiritual in nature. The journey of the Warrior is to find the balance between the rage and rationality, between being impulsive and calm/composed. A Warrior, however, will also create conflict when there is no conflict. If there is no Dragon, there is not a need for a Warrior.

At first, the Warrior may go overboard. The Warrior sees everything as a Dragon and thinks everyone needs rescuing. One analogy is "if the only tool you have is a hammer, then everything looks like a nail." (Abraham Maslow, from "The Psychology of Science" (1966)). If you can picture a pendulum, when one goes from Orphan to Warrior, the pendulum may be making a great swing at first. We may rage and annihilate the Dragon that perhaps only needs talking to. Anger, though, can be a healthy motivator in and of itself if that anger is acted out in a way that is healthy or appropriate. The energy from anger helps us move forward.

The Warrior sees everything as a contest with a winner and a loser. The Warrior needs the teachings of the Martyr. According to Carol Pearson (1986) page 76, if the Warrior has not taken the journey into the Martyr state, then the journey is stuck in an us/them mindset.

A Warrior is intuitive and has sharp/keen instincts. A balanced Warrior is very aware of and in tune with their body and learns how to stand and face situations with courage and reclaim power that was taken in childhood. Healthy boundaries keep us safe and assist us in knowing where we end, and another begins. In the Warrior archetype, we learn what helps us, nourishes us, and what really needs slaying or letting go of. Boundaries are a statement of self-respect. We can only stop disrespectful behaviour from others after we have stopped treating ourselves disrespectfully.

ABANDONMENT AND THE WARRIOR ARCHETYPE

I have thought about this segment for quite a while. In fact, a deep struggle ensued for me, which I will share more of when I discuss my personal experiences later in the chapter.

The out of balance/pseudo-Warrior is the Abandoner — the Abandoner of self who is very fear based.

Even when we are in balance, there is going to be grief events in our lives, and we will SWIRL through the stages. We will experience grief and loss because we have dreams, hopes, and plans, and when there is a breaking of an attachment, there is abandonment grief.

The healthier we are, the more we heal our wounds, the easier it is to manage SWIRL and not have Chuckee be the ruler of our lives and relationships. We can feel the feeling of fear and act from our Big or frontal lobe. We no longer need to defend just because we feel fear. We still experience the stages of SWIRL and we manage ourselves differently, less reactionary, in each stage.

SWIRL

Shattering

The words that come to mind for this Warrior Archetype are, "What if I lose the fight?" "What if I am not good enough to win?" The shock that it could be true that I might not be good enough urges me to fight harder, conquer more. The belief is "I must prove myself, and if I don't, then I have lost all. What if I don't see the Dragon and they get me?"

Withdrawal

Withdrawal can occur for the Warrior when there is a calm. In a state of calm, the adrenaline level is lowered, and we experience a withdrawal from adrenaline. Also, there is a withdrawal from the routine of being in conflict, which is a disruption in a familiar pattern. A backlash from an outburst can also leave us in a state of feeling scared and wanting contact, wanting to reconnect/attach. We experience tension arising from the compulsion to repeat a pattern and return to a familiar state.

Internalizing the Rejection

The Warrior Archetype becomes the Hero, slaying or converting the Dragon, thus, rescuing the Victim. The toxic Warrior can also play the Villian role. In the journey through internalizing, the Warrior understands that the failure, or the not winning, as shared in shattering, is their own fault. This dynamic creates a feeling of shame causing the toxic Warrior to become the Villian, slaying Dragons rather than processing feelings of shame.

For the out-of-balance Warrior, when feeling threatened, there is blame toward anybody or anything. The language of this blame might sound like, "They were just lying," "they just wanted to get me fired." The internal examination does not happen for the out-of-balance Warrior. In a healthy Warrior, there is an examination of who the Dragon is and how best to proceed based on integrity and knowing the self. Believing that oneself is not good enough can lead to outward lashing in rage rather than facing the internalized belief and making an internal change. Sometimes the Dragon is internal, it is us.

Rage

For the healthy Warrior, rage plays the role of providing the energy and motivation to go forward to right the wrong, to speak for the downtrodden, to speak to injustices and demand fairness. This is called moral outrage and gives us the fire in the belly to drive us to action. In the out-of-balance Warrior, rage seeks to destroy anything that may expose an underbelly or pose as a threat, real or imagined. The fear of loss of autonomy will incite rage.

Lifting

Lifting can be experienced in the healthy Warrior when change is occurring. Change which will bring about inclusion and fairness and offer hope. Change can be fear-filled. All change brings with it facets of the unknown, and we like to be in control; so, we want to stay in the familiar so it feels like we can know what will happen, which is actually an illusion of control.

Lifting in an out-of-balance Warrior can be seen as moving on to conquer the next Dragon without witnessing any fallout or ramifications of the previous slaying or discovering the root cause of the pattern.

SHARON'S PERSONAL EXPERIENCE OF THE WARRIOR ARCHETYPE

Well, I certainly know the pendulum swing from Orphan to Warrior. I can still swing a pretty wide arc; however, I do not do so often and not for any length of time now. I come back to rest in a fairly balanced state quite quickly. I refer to what I used to do as swathing. It is a farming term referring to the act of cutting hay into windrows to dry quicker. I imagine a machine cutting down whatever is in the way of making that row. Everything to me was a Dragon; I was the potential damsel in distress, the one who had never been rescued. No one had ever rescued me, so I was rescuing myself before anyone could even come close to hurting me. I was keeping me safe. I made conflict where there wasn't any, I hurt people, and, for the most part, I did not take my Wanderer journey, so I hurt myself, repeating patterns, which kept me in the Orphan and Martyr archetypes.

So, as I stated before, this chapter has been the most difficult for me. I have been challenged by each chapter and have healed and embraced the many gifts I have received from each step of the journey so far. The gift in this chapter that I am aware of goes once again back to the Mahatma Gandhi name calling. What a legacy, what a gift. The gift I received from this name calling, was knowing I had values, integrity, and that I had a voice before I was wounded.

I really believed this chapter would be a snap for me, while Kathy believed she would really struggle because she did not see herself as a Warrior, although I see her as a great Warrior. I thought I was a Warrior throughout my life—breaking intergenerational patterns, receiving an education, and single parenting, to name a few accomplishments. Perhaps I did accomplish these things; however, I did not do so in the healthiest of ways. As I examined each situation through the lens of the Warrior, what I encountered was a slice of the pseudo-Warrior and rage. I railed against the fact that I was in these positions of "having" to do it all on my own. This Orphan state was so reminiscent of growing up with emotionally absent/abusive parents and abusive teachers who betrayed me that I had internalized their beliefs and behaviours. I had become my parents and the teachers toward myself without even realizing what I was doing. I recreated the trauma. The only way I could rescue/protect myself at that time was through rage. These actions are defensive actions (Chuckee) and a trauma response. This dynamic hurt my children immensely. Sometimes they became the Dragons to be slain. Unfortunately, my actions were very hurtful, and they carry the scars and wounds.

I am still quick to react when I think someone wants something from me, (sensitivity rejection) has expectations about what I will or will not do or interferes with my autonomy. I can, for the most part, slow the process down and separate out the past (then) and the present (now) so that I respond as an adult (frontal lobe) and with appropriate boundaries.

I did take some of my Warrior journey and I did slay some Dragons that needed to be slain. I broke generational patterns, whether as a trauma response or not. I continue to heal, take my journey, and recognize Dragons to be slain and Dragons to be acknowledged as they subside.

I do not swath anymore, and I do not "read" a room to know where the Dragons are so I can "get" them before they get me. I know from experience that I will manage myself in each moment or situation. If I abandon myself, I also know I am very capable of returning to the scene and owning my behaviour and acknowledging that I created my own consequences.

SHARON'S PERSONAL EXPERIENCE OF SCRIPTURE WITH THE WARRIOR ARCHETYPE

I know that Warrior God (El Shaddai) has rescued me and stood for me more times that I can ever be aware of. I know He wants me to stand for Him also. I can do that more now as my healing deepens and my faith is exercised (Psalm 18).

I know too that the Holy Spirit is my "swather". The Holy Spirit goes before me and makes a clear path (Deuteronomy 31:8). I very rarely push the boulder up a hill. No matter how big the circumstance, God never fails me (Psalm 86:10).

I have struggled to be able to speak my truth. Fear of the outcome, silenced by the belief I did not have anything of value to say, and at times not even knowing what my truth was, kept me silent and disassociated in many situations. I was either quiet or raging. With healing and God's grace, I am quiet when I need to be and appropriately (most of the time) angry when I need to be. Luke 12:12 says, "for the Holy Spirit will teach you at that time what you should say." The Holy Spirit will give me words to say at the moment I need them.

My pattern was to judge and make the other wrong. Scripture tells me that God is the judge of everyone, as in Isaiah 33:22, I am quickly learning (quick for me) that I am safe whether I am right, and they are wrong, or I am wrong, and they are right. My job description has changed as I slay the Dragons, let go, heal, and rest in God.

I experience being given words or the wisdom or insight frequently when facilitating group sessions. While listening to group members discussing and sharing personal experiences, sometimes I provide an answer to someone's question, and later, when someone refers back to that answer, I realize I have no idea what I said. I have no memory of forming that particular thought and I don't even know from where I would get the information. Perhaps a few days later the information surfaces to conscious level.

In the Warrior sections, I spoke of trauma responses and breaking patterns. While I was surviving, my motive for breaking the patterns was not from a healed, heathy place. God used all of it for His good. The tools He has given me to respond rather than react are ones of compassion to allow me to see past the behaviour, to be able to understand my own and the others' actions, and to have discernment, which enables me to separate out feelings from the past from those of the present. I can stay grounded and more present most of the time.

My daily prayer is to keep me safe and keep others and myself safe from me. God is patient and full of grace. I am learning.

HOW DO FAITH AND GOD'S WORD INTERSECT WITH THE WARRIOR ARCHETYPE? (KATHY)

"For though we live in the world, we do not wage war as the world does. The weapons we fight with are not the weapons of the world. On the contrary, they have divine power to demolish strongholds. We demolish arguments and every pretension that sets itself up against the knowledge of God, and we take captive every thought to make it obedient to Christ."

—2 Corinthians: 10:3–5

The Warrior archetype is accepted and taken very seriously by people of faith as it pertains to the spiritual battles between good and evil. The Bible is very clear that when confronted with evil, we must put on the full armour of God.

Therefore, put on the full armor of God, so that when the day of evil comes, you may be able to stand your ground, and after you have done everything, to stand. Stand firm then, with the belt of truth buckled around your waist, with the breastplate of righteousness in place, and with your feet fitted with the readiness that comes from the gospel of peace. In addition to all this, take up the shield of faith, with which you can extinguish all the flaming arrows of the evil one. Take the helmet of salvation and the sword of the Spirit, which is the word of God. And pray in the Spirit on all occasions with all kinds of prayers and requests. With this in mind, be alert and always keep on praying for all the Lord's people. (Ephesians 6:13–18)

Despite these strong verses, when we are confronted with the Warrior archetype in ourselves, many in the faith-based community struggle. For one thing, the Bible says to turn the other cheek (Matthew 5:38–40). How can that be reconciled to the Warrior in each one of us?

The Warrior archetype might be more aptly described as the overcomer or the hero battling for righteousness led by the wisdom of the Bible and the Holy Spirit. Of course, some Warriors do fight physical battles with the weapons of war against physical enemies, but even during these times of war, Christ followers must be aware that the outcome of every battle belongs to the Lord. The Bible says in 2 Samuel 10:12, "Be strong, and let us fight bravely for our people and the cities of our God. The Lord will do what is good in his sight." We do our best and trust God's love and His will in all things.

The Warrior archetype does not always fight physical foes with concrete weaponry. Warriors often battle injustice or battle to protect themselves while setting boundaries to ensure safety from personal abuse or the abuse of others. Personal value or the intrinsic value of others is often at stake. Sometimes the battles of the Warrior archetype are internal and require metaphysical weapons and assertiveness.

The ultimate battle for Christ followers is the spiritual war against Satan and his realm, the battle of good and evil. Satan is the father of lies (John 8:44), telling us lies about ourselves and others, stirring us up one against another, "For our struggle is not against flesh and blood, but against the rulers, against the authorities, against the powers of this dark world and against the spiritual forces of evil in the heavenly realms" (Ephesians 6:12). Our challenge is to use our Warrior energies to fight the good fight against evil while relying on God and His Word for wisdom and direction and trusting that He is in control of the outcome. God is the overcomer!

The purest example of the Warrior archetype is Jesus himself. He said He had come to divide families with the sword of scripture (Luke 12:51). He was outraged by the money changers misuse of the temple (Matthew 21:12) and He had very strong criticism for the Pharisees

(Luke 11:52). However, His most significant and fierce battle is a spiritual one, as described in 1 John 3:8: "The one who does what is sinful is of the devil, because the devil has been sinning from the beginning. The reason the Son of God appeared was to destroy the devil's work."

An example of the Warrior archetype in the Old Testament is found in the book of Daniel, Chapter 3. Here we read the story of Shadrach, Meshach, and Abednego. These three Hebrew men refused to worship foreign gods or to bow down to the image of Nebuchadnezzar, the king of Babylon, and in punishment they were thrown into a fiery furnace. All three men escaped harm, and the king saw not three but four men walking in the flames. The Bible says in Daniel 3:25, "Look! I see four men walking around in the fire, unbound and unharmed, and the fourth looks like a son of the gods."

Shadrach, Meshach, and Abednego stood firm and strong, obeying God's Word in the face of extreme danger and what appeared to be imminent death. When commanded by the king to worship the gods of Babylon and his own golden image,

> Shadrach, Meshach, and Abednego replied to him, "King Nebuchadnezzar, we do not need to defend ourselves before you in this matter. If we are thrown into the blazing furnace, the God we serve is able to deliver us from it, and he will deliver us from Your Majesty's hand. But even if he does not, we want you to know, Your Majesty, that we will not serve your gods or worship the image of gold you have set up." (Daniel 3:16)

They were overcomers refusing to bow to the bullying of the king.

In the New Testament, we read the story of Paul, another Warrior/overcomer. Before his conversion, Paul, then known as Saul, zealously persecuted the Christians. He stood firm in his faith as a Pharisee, but afterwards he fought without regard to his personal safety or comfort to spread the Word and advance the cause of Christ. Paul admits his past and explains his mission to the people of Galatia:

For you have heard of my previous way of life in Judaism, how intensely I persecuted the church of God and tried to destroy it. I was advancing in Judaism beyond many of my own age among my people and was extremely zealous for the traditions of my fathers. But when God, who set me apart from my mother's womb and called me by his grace, was pleased to reveal his Son in me so that I might preach him among the Gentiles, my immediate response was not to consult any human being. (Galatians 1:13–16)

Always a Warrior in his spirit and steadfast in his beliefs, Saul/Paul, committed to a new life and a new passion, the good news of eternal life with Jesus.

There are many other examples of overcomers in the Bible, men and women called to stand firm for Jesus and God's Word, doing what is right and good in the face of tremendous odds against them as they rely on the wisdom and direction of the Holy Spirit. The ways and means vary greatly, but all stand up with razor sharp focus, intelligence, courage, acute intuition, and creative Warrior energy. I offer these words of God to his Warriors in closing:

Have I not commanded you? Be strong and courageous. Do not be afraid; do not be discouraged, for the Lord your God will be with you wherever you go.

(Joshua 1:9)

Kathy's personal Experience with the Warrior Archetype

"Fear not, for I am with you; be not dismayed,
for I am your God; I will strengthen you,
I will help you, I will uphold you with my righteous right hand."
—Isaiah 41:10

Original drawing by Verna Bulled is entitled "Man Versus His Demons".

Everyone faces demons, challenges, and Dragons every day, and we face them in many ways, whether by standing firm and fighting or with the staff of the Wanderer, making our way through by trial and error. The cross, symbol of our faith, separates us from every demon and leads us back to the face of peace. We always walk with the Lord: "I am with you always, to the very end of the age" (Matthew 28:20).

As Sharon wrote earlier in this chapter, the goal of the Warrior archetype is to slay the Dragon that was named by the Wanderer, and an important question is, "Who is the Dragon?" That is a very good question! When the Warrior archetype is active within me, sometimes everyone and everything appears to be a Dragon to be slain. Sometimes I don't know who or what the Dragon is, but intuitively, I know he's out there!

The story of my experience with cancer is not complete without the Warrior's part. My oncologist, a wonderful, wise, and caring doctor, said that my fighting spirit was my best tool and ultimate weapon to deal with the disease. In hindsight, I know this was true, but at the beginning of the journey, I could not find my Dragon, so who was I fighting? I mistook the technicians that measured my body for radiation as the Dragon. I mistook the receptionist at the doctor's office for the Dragon. I sometimes even mistook my family for the Dragon when they did not agree with my decisions. Finally, as I wandered through literature about different religions, practiced various forms of meditation, studied books about nutrition and even more books about the mind/body/spirit connection, I realized that the cancer eating at my body was my ferocious and deadly Dragon. Once focused on the battle and the foe, I could choose my weapons!

I knew that God could detour my path at any time, and I knew deep in my soul that He was with me at every step. With the weapon of faith and truth, I prayed endlessly. Scripture says, "And pray in the Spirit on all occasions with all kinds of prayers and requests. With this in mind, be alert and always keep on praying for all the Lord's people" (Ephesians 6:18). I was confident in the process because in Mark 11:24,

I read, "Therefore I tell you, whatever you ask in prayer, believe that you have received it, and it will be yours."

I trusted my doctors and caregivers (most of the time), took medications as prescribed, carefully weighed information, and prayerfully made decisions about treatment. When I was undergoing radiation, I sang, "God is so Good." The radiologist would tease me because he said he could tell how anxious I was on any given day by the number of times I was able to sing the chorus during my treatment. Of course, it was true that the more nervous I was the faster I sang.

I wielded the weapon of knowledge by eating carefully every day. Mindful of antioxidants, complete proteins, and vitamins and minerals, I held on to the verses in 1 Corinthians 6:19–20, "Do you not know that your bodies are temples of the Holy Spirit, who is in you, whom you have received from God? You are not your own; you were bought at a price. Therefore, honor God with your bodies." Meditation was another weapon. I meditated on the Word of God and practiced Creative Visualization because Paul says, "Do not be conformed to this world, but be transformed by the renewing of your mind, that by testing you may discern what is the will of God, what is good and acceptable and perfect" (Romans 12:2). Finally, through my research I learned that laughing, watching comedies and "feel good" movies, could raise my endorphin level so I used humour as a paradoxical weapon while I trusted in Proverbs 17:22, "A cheerful heart is good medicine, but a crushed spirit dries up the bones."

I worked at resting in the Lord, staying positive as much as possible and fighting hard to improve my health. In my heart of hearts, I thank Him for walking with me every step of every day and picking me up whenever I fell or became discouraged: "The Lord is my strength and my shield; my heart trusts in him, and he helps me. My heart leaps for joy, and with my song I praise him" (Psalm 28:7).

I called up my inner Warrior archetype to fight the good fight with my cancer. I did not use guns or arrows but faith, knowledge, discipline, and the strength of my God. When I was discouraged or too weak to fight, I rested my whole being in God's right hand because I knew that He would hold me up. My Warrior archetype with the strength of God did not defeat cancer, but I am in remission, and I am richer and wiser in my spirit because of the fight! When the Warrior archetype does not arm itself with weapons but with faith and prayer while relying on the "renewing of the mind" and God's "good and perfect will" (Romans 12:2), lives are transformed.

CHAPTER FIVE

The Magician
(Sharon)

IN THE MAGICIAN Archetype the journey is one of transformation, trust, and alignment with a power greater than us. SWIRL becomes less until there is a need (fear) for one of the other archetypes.

Goal of the Magician: According to Pearson, the goal of the Magician is to live in harmony with the supernatural and natural worlds by creating and re-creating, transforming ourselves as an ever-evolving state. We learn that we are part of the unfolding of God. We learn we are responsible for our lives, the choices we make, the consequences of those choices, and the life we create.

Goad in Abandonment: Goal is to always remain open and in the moment.

Toxic Magician: One who has not taken the journey of the Orphan, Martyr, or Wanderer or who has unresolved Warrior issues and so does not know the self. The toxic Magician uses the tools of the Magician as a weapon of destruction. A state of superiority and power over.

The Orphan will want to be magically rescued instead of doing the work of rescuing the self.

Pearson says, the Martyr will be giving the wrong gifts at the wrong time to the wrong people if the journey of discovery of self worth and purpose has not been resolved. We will give ourselves and our gifts based on who we think we should be, rather than who we are. Who we think we should be can change with each person we are with because we base our acceptable identity on who we think others want us to be. This is an old, learned way of Chuckee thinking. This behaviour was to keep Little safe, while in reality it now keeps Little stuck.

The Wanderer will be asking if this is the right decision, the right path, rather than taking the steps and discovering the path and then walking down the path. This self-doubt is Chuckee, sabotaging us because Little is fearful of the upcoming changes and Big has not soothed but rather given in to fear.

The Warrior will want some magic to know what Dragon is the one to slay and so, not knowing, the out-of-balance Warrior will use the Magician tools as a weapon of destruction.

As a Magician, we must give our lives fully surrendered to the universe believing that our gifts are exactly the right ones (Pearson). Magicians embrace the world as a place of wonder, amazement, and beauty and find themselves in a friendly home-like place. This is different than the other archetypes, which experience the world as a fear-filled place with obstacles to overcome. The Magician thusly reclaims the Innocent archetype.

The Magician learns through relationships that they can trust themselves and so becomes aware that they are part of the mysterious workings of God.

In the Magician archetype, we learn that we are not victims of life, and depending on our journey, how we learn to give or take, we co-create with God. How we do our archetypal journey determines the part we play in this unfolding. Another way of phrasing this would be to say that how many wounds we have healed, how emotionally mature we are, and how we have embraced situations and allowed them to age/mature us is the degree to which we will increase our resiliency and assist in our role in the unfolding of God in the universe.

Magicians do not force change as perhaps the Warrior might. The Magician knows that the action which will move forward is one of disciplined clarity and caring and strength of will, along with and because of the supernatural power at work. Magicians live being true to themselves in each moment.

The Magician believes that Grace is one kind of transforming energy available to us and that we are co-creators of change. We must do our part (surrender or not) and take the consequences for all outcomes of our decisions and actions, either favourable or not.

The Magician archetype requires us to take responsibility for all our parts, which includes the toxic (shadow) side. This means we embrace rather than blame or slay these parts of ourselves, hence life is seen as a process, neither good nor bad. When we repress or negate parts of ourselves, they tend to grow in the dark and manifest in an unhealthy way. All parts are acceptable; it is the behaviour out of these parts that creates difficulty. When we embrace or accept these parts, we can then choose how we are going to respond or manage our behaviour and remain in a more balanced (regulated) state.

Living in this way is an example of being in the moment. We learn to stay attuned to what is going on around us and, most importantly, inside us. When parts, instead of behaviours, are labelled and rejected, then we feel shame and hide these parts in order not to be rejected. So, we reject ourselves by only showing those parts we have learned are acceptable, and the repressed parts fester and break out in reactionary behaviour creating more hurt and regret (this is Chuckee behaviour, and a survival state). When we repeat this cycle, we return to the Orphan and Martyr archetype and then move into the toxic Warrior archetype in order to defend ourselves instead of moving toward the Magician archetype. We loop or cycle back to and continue the familiar patterns.

As we embrace these wounded parts, heal, and mature, we discover that we do not use those once-often-called-upon coping tools. We are in the process of becoming more of the person we choose or were meant to be, rather than a reactionary victim. We are in the process of growing a larger us. This is a process of re-wiring the neuropathways of the brain, creating more resiliency.

For example, women especially have learned that we are to be "nice," which means repressing our assertive nature. In the Magician archetype, we travel the road of learning and transforming the behaviour of "nice" into caring assertiveness. The caring starts with caring for the self, which in turn translates into caring for others by being assertive and honest in relationships. One can be "nice" and assertive at the same time. Being "nice" does not exclude other feelings such as frustration or anger. To break this social norm takes courage and can provoke anxiety in the face of perhaps being rejected by another, which is hurtful. However, being rejected by another is less harmful than being rejected by the self. To act courageously or bravely involves taking a risk. We may pray, in what ever way we do, for the ability to act or the strength to do the act, and then we have it and do it. This is faith at work, transforming us step by step. Having what we need when we need it is an underlying precept of the Magician archetype. In the Magician archetype, we take on life's opportunities and challenges with purpose, which in turn fills us with life and vitality and transforms us.

As we journey through the archetypes, we learn how to be free from attachments, either to ideas, things, or people. Our overreliance, our need for others to meet all of our needs creates a dependency which in turn keeps us chained. When we break the shackles of attachment, we become more reliant on God (whatever that is for you), which creates more interdependence. This may seem like a paradox, a substituting of one chain for another. There is a marked difference. The Magician is ruled from a place of love and caring, and choices are made from this position rather than a position of emotional fear. We choose God because we love and are now able to choose how we can be the best us we can be with the assistance of God. We no longer serve man but God. Who were we created to be? We are now free to explore this new terrain.

This journey of embracing the previously unacceptable parts and naming them as part of self is the journey toward wholeness. The more healed we are, the more mature we are. The more mature we are, the more we act instead of react. We are more resilient, and while we still experience all the disappointments and sadness life holds, we "bounce back" more easily. We have more ability to "see" in a very insightful way. Situations take on different meanings and values than they held when we were in any of the other archetypes. We have been transformed and we in turn transform the world around us.

ABANDONMENT IN THE MAGICIAN ARCHETYPE

The SWIRL is not a big factor in the life of Magician in the same manner it is in the other archetypes. Because our brain is hardwired to danger/safety, our brain does become flooded with chemicals like adrenaline to alert us and ready us to survive. The Magician very quickly determines whether the threat is based on a real and present danger/ threat or a perceived threat that may be based on past experiences. The Magician recognizes old familiar patterns and consciously changes thinking and then the feelings change. This in turn allows for access to the frontal lobe of the brain to find an action we consider appropriate. This is the resiliency I spoke of in the preceding paragraph. This process creates new neuropathways in the brain/re-wires the brain. In the Magician archetype, we rewrite the script of memories from an aged place or a wise place or from the adult part of us, transforming the memories which were given meaning by a much younger self.

There is less need for Chuckee in the Magician archetype as the role for Chuckee is diminished because the need to be defended has decreased. Remember, Chuckee is only present when there is a need to defend against a perceived emotional threat which creates fear of rejection or loss in Little. We may for a brief moment find our self in the Orphan or Martyr archetype; however, it seems these jaunts are short-lived and not as intense.

Sharon's Personal Experience of Scripture with the Magician Archetype

"If anyone hears my words but does not keep them, I do not judge that person. For I did not come to judge the world, but to save the world. There is a judge for the one who rejects me and does not accept my words; the very words I have spoken will condemn them at the last day. For I did not speak on my own, but the Father who sent me commanded me to say all that I have spoken. I know that his command leads to eternal life. So whatever I say is just what the Father has told me to say."

—John 12: 47–50

Our role is to surrender to the notion that God wants good for us, surrender to wanting what God wants more than what we want. Sometimes they even turn out to be the same things. Surrendering requires trust, willingness, and faith, faith we already have within us. When we have chosen to surrender and align with God, our experiences inform us that God is present and working in our life. The process of surrendering allows us to see with different eyes, perhaps the eyes of the heart. From this new perspective, change occurs. The lies of our history are being undone and transformation occurs.

I can see transformation in my own life when I can open my heart, which means risking, being vulnerable, trusting, having faith, and being willing to see differently instead of being caught up in fear based on my past and lies. Following this transformation, I saw my youngest brother in a new light or with open eyes. Over days, I could feel my heart open, transforming. I saw the brother I knew when he was five years old. He was caring, innocent, and willing. As I was becoming more willing to let go of my old beliefs about my brother, I was transformed by the Holy Spirit, becoming a co-creator of a new me. I still struggle with wanting him to "get it." And I can at times still feel resentment toward him for not planning, not getting it right. God is teaching me by allowing me to see that I have this need to be right, and when I am in this mental/emotional state, I fight like my life depends on it. Maybe I did have to do this when I was younger because if I missed an external clue, then I was blindsided and not prepared to defend myself from abuse.

The other side of this pattern is that I want my brother to be wrong, and not only wrong, but to admit he is wrong. God is healing this part of me, and I can, more often than not, allow my brother to be himself and also allow me to be me. I do not need to defend. Our relationship is taking on a dynamic based more on caring about rather than caretaking. I bet he is so relieved. He is so gracious; God is using my brother in a very miraculous way.

God is my defense; therefore, I have no need to be defended. Psalm 3:3 tells me "You, oh Lord, are the shield around me." My relationship with my brother has changed like night and day. My relationship with myself has also changed through the transformation of this sibling relationship. This transformation then ripples out to other relationships.

I learned it is not my role to teach, train, correct, or mold others. Yes, children we teach and guide. In this context, I am speaking about our adult relationships. In adult relationships, my only role, as I see it, is to love others without a specific recipe for that love. Because God is my defender, I have no need to fear or guard (I'm not saying I never end up in that mindset; I am saying there is no need for it). We all will answer one day for our lives and the choices we have made. Paraphrased, John 12:47–50 says that even I (meaning Jesus) do not judge you. I (Jesus) came into the world to save you so you could be free. My (Jesus') Father in heaven is the One who will judge all one day.

I struggle at times with the notion that God loves me and wants good for me, which means He will change me and act through me. I have come to realize that I have a deep-seated belief that I will be punished or rejected if I become excited or joy-filled at the changes in myself or if I share what I believe God is doing in my life. This is rooted in my mother's name for me, Mahatma Gandhi—arrogant, superior singled out. According to God's Word, I am singled out, I am chosen like all other Children whom God has chosen to call. This does not mean I am arrogant or superior. John 15:5 says Jesus is the vine and I am the branches. A branch cannot bear fruit on its own. The branch must remain in Jesus. Remembering this verse helps keep me humble.

I have experienced some powerful transformations over my life. Each one occurred when I was willing to confess that I had come to the end of myself and to recognize I needed God because I could not do what I knew was the right thing to do. The transformation was instantaneous. If I was holding on to one particle, meaning I was not fully surrendered, then I remained in the situation. Only when I was fully surrendered, without a "yeah, but," without any fear, was God able to transform me. Only after I had fully done my part was God free to transform me. God also gave me the courage and the words to say and do what I needed to do. In fact, there wasn't any fear. The way/path was very clear. What I know to be true from His word is that while I have been forgiven, I still have consequences, some in this life and some to account for come the day I stand before Him.

I experience all the disappointment and shattering of rejection and loss the same as everyone else as that is the human condition. Through

God's transforming power I am more resilient and can experience these feelings and have these experiences without the devastation which once accompanied them.

I thank God daily for saving me, for never leaving me, for being my strength and shield, always providing and loving me and teaching me to love. I also thank God for putting counsellors in my life, whether they were Christian or secular. All had a part in my healing.

God has given me many songs over the years, such as "I'll Take the Next Step," "A Little Slice of Heaven," "The Seeker Healer," "I Cry Out To You," and many more. I am forever grateful for this gift.

As I finish this chapter, I am sitting in a cottage in the middle of a forest. I have taken two weeks off to recharge and regroup. The last two years have been stressful and filled with so many learning and healing moments. My daughters are monitoring my brother; one has taken time from work and the other will spell her off when needed. I am so grateful.

I am healing from PTSD and from a concussion experienced in a fall two years ago. There isn't anyone for a few kilometers. No people or traffic noise. My self-talk is interesting. My physical body responses are enlightening. My mind says, "You can call someone to have a conversation. "What I do instead is check in with Little and soothe without calling someone. My body says we should be doing something. I check in with Little and address the message about feeling lazy. I stay still.

When I was out walking this morning, which was somewhat spooky, as there may be bears or cougars out there, my mind was saying we should go in and write now. Then I asked myself what I really wanted to do. The answer, accompanied by joy, was stay out and walk! I was experiencing the dynamic of joy being closely associated with the idea that "bad" things will happen if I allow this joy state to continue. Well, I stayed out and nothing "bad" happened; I am sitting here writing. Very interesting.

One cannot be in joy and guarded at the same time. What I can do, though, is be in joy and remain aware. I can have joy and retain the knowledge that I have many tools, including prayer, and I am safe. This is an example of being in the Magician archetype, transforming fear into love.

How Do Faith and God's Word Intersect with the Magician Archetype? (Kathy)

"Therefore, if anyone is in Christ, the new creation has come:
The old has gone, the new is here!"
2 Corinthians 5:17

The Bible has much to say about magicians, and none of it good (Exodus 22:18; Leviticus 20:27), but the archetype of the Magician is very different from the magician that administers potions, casts spells, and foretells the future. The Magician, from a faith-based perspective, is the archetype that calls on inner psychic, supernatural, intuitive knowledge and the power of God. The Magician archetype appears within a mature faith-based believer as they surrender to God and allow themselves to be transformed to be more like Jesus himself (Romans 8:29). The difference between the magician, worker of magic, and the Magician archetype in the context of God's Word is the transformative power of the Holy Spirit!

When discussing the Magician archetype in the context of the Bible, it is important to realize that the Bible is God's story written for our learning, not man's story written for man's understanding. God is the centre of the story. It is difficult to discern what the characters in the Bible are thinking or how their minds are processing and working. We read about their relationship to God and God's faithfulness to believers.

As a believer, I can put myself in a magical position by trusting God and allowing Him to be the transforming agent in my life. When I accept Christ as my Saviour, He dwells within me (Galatians 2:20). My role is to surrender my life and my will to God and ask him to give me wisdom and direction. Proverbs 3:5–6 says, "Trust in the Lord with all your heart and lean not on your own understanding; in all your ways submit to him, and he will make your paths straight." I can trust in the Lord because he says I can in Jeremiah 29:11. "For I know the plans I have for you, plans to prosper you and not to harm you, plans to give you hope and a future". My hope is in the Lord (Isaiah 40:31) and I know that nothing is impossible for Him (Luke 1:37).

Have you heard the saying, "When life gives you lemons, make lemonade" (a common idiom based on a quote from Elbert Hubbard). In my opinion, this typifies the archetype of the Magician, except I might interpret it as, "When life gives you hardships and troubles, give them to God in prayer, asking for His transformative power." Not nearly as memorable, but in a faith-based community, the archetype of the Magician appears as we walk with Jesus and mature in the faith through the power of the Holy Spirit. "And we all, who with unveiled faces contemplate the Lord's glory, are being transformed into his image with ever-increasing glory, which comes from the Lord, who is the Spirit" (2 Corinthians 3:18). The source of the transforming power to make "lemonade" out of us comes from God.

The world is always changing and evolving, and each one of us is changing and evolving along with it. The Bible says that we work along side Christ: "For we are co-workers in God's service; you are God's field, God's building" (1 Corinthians 3:9). He made us (Psalm 139:13–14), and He only wants the best for us (Psalm 37:4). God created each one of us for a purpose, "For we are God's handiwork, created in Christ Jesus to do good works, which God prepared in advance for us to do" (Ephesians 2:10). As a believer, God is my centre, not myself. The Magician archetype will manifest itself when I surrender and trust in Him.

Examples of the Magician archetype working through the charac-ters in the Bible are numerous and illustrate the workings of the Holy

Trinity—God, Jesus and the Holy Spirit. Moses uses the Magician archetype when he leads his people, the Israelites, away from their Egyptian captors to the promised land (Exodus). Daniel is saved from hungry lions when God's power is manifested through the miraculous "shutting of the lions mouths" (Daniel 6:22) Joseph's story, found in Genesis 37–47, is another that exemplifies the Magician archetype. Due to jealousy and deceit, Joseph's brothers sold him into slavery and Joseph found himself a house servant in the household of an assistant to the Pharaoh of Egypt, Potiphar. However, "The Lord was with Joseph so that he prospered, and he lived in the house of his Egyptian master" (Genesis 39:2). Potiphar soon put him in charge of everything he owned. However, through lies and deceit Joseph found himself in King Pharaoh's prison with Pharaoh's baker and cupbearer. Through the power of God, he was able to correctly interpret the cupbearer's dream and he asked that the cupbearer when released would tell Pharaoh about him.

One day, Pharaoh had a dream that no one could interpret. His cupbearer immediately remembered Joseph and told Pharaoh about him. Pharaoh then asked Joseph if he could interpret dreams. Joseph gave the glory to God. He told Pharaoh that he, himself, could not understand dreams, but God helped him. Through the interpretation of Pharaoh's dreams, Joseph was again placed in a position of power. He was put in charge of all the food in the country of Egypt. Joseph came up with a plan to save Egypt from severe famine. When Joseph's family was starving, they traveled to Egypt for food. Through a series of events and a fascinating story, Joseph forgave his brothers for selling him into slavery and helped his family find a home and work in Egypt. Joseph was relying on God, and God manifested his transformative power through Joseph. Not that bad things didn't happen to Joseph, but with God he was able to rise above his circumstances and focus on the work at hand. Joseph could not have foreseen how God was transforming his life. The Magician archetype was at work in him and in every situation, Joseph was successful and blessed.

The most dramatic example of the Magician archetype is found in Jesus. There is no lack of miracles in the life of Jesus from his conception as the son of God (Matthew 1:18–25) to his death on the cross (Matthew 27:32–56) and his subsequent resurrection (Luke 24:1–12). Another way Jesus shows us the power of God through the Magician archetype is through his miracles. Jesus heals the sick (e.g., Healing of a man born blind, John 1:9–12), raises the dead (e.g., Lazarus was raised from the dead, John 11:1–44), and exorcises demons (e.g., Casting a demon from a man in the synagogue, Mark 1:22–27). Jesus also shows his miraculous power over nature. He turns water to wine at a wedding (John 2:1–11) and commands a miraculous catch of fish from the Sea of Galilee (Luke 5:1–8). He feeds the multitude by changing five loaves of bread and two fishes into enough food to feed a multitude of people (Matthew 14:13–21). Jesus walks on the surface of the water and with faith the apostle Peter walks out towards him (Matthew 14:22–33). In a ferocious storm, Jesus calms the storm by "rebuking" the wind and waves (Mark 4:35–41). There are other miracles too numerous and some too complicated to explain here. However, I believe Jesus clearly demonstrated God's power and might through his physical body.

The miraculous, the supernatural, the magical power of the Magician archetype is demonstrated in biblical times, but also in today's world through believers and the work of the Holy Spirit. The power of faith as tiny as a mustard seed can move mountains (Matthew 17:20). Through prayer and the strength of the Almighty God anything is possible. The Magician archetype will surface when you submit to the Lord and allow his saving grace to give you lemonade in place of the lemons that you have created for yourself. God will provide for you and not turn you away:

> Then Jesus declared, "I am the bread of life. Whoever comes to me will never go hungry, and whoever believes in me will never be thirsty. But as I told you, you have seen me and still you do not believe. All those the Father gives

me will come to me, and whoever comes to me I will never drive away. For I have come down from heaven not to do my will but to do the will of him who sent me. And this is the will of him who sent me, that I shall lose none of all those he has given me but raise them up at the last day. For my Father's will is that everyone who looks to the Son and believes in him shall have eternal life, and I will raise them up at the last day." (John 6:35–40)

KATHY'S PERSONAL EXPERIENCE OF THE MAGICIAN ARCHETYPE

Dreams shatter! Circumstances change! Life eventually throws out a lemon or two! When someone lives well despite the "lemons of life," others label them survivors. I think we survive when we do what we must do to live the preferred future God has planned for us. I think of survival more like learning a series of life lessons and completing the challenges given to me to accomplish God's plan for my life. He knows what I need, what will make me happy, and what he has enabled me to do. For the most part, I have learned not to go out on my own strength but to wait on the Lord for opportunities to accomplish His plans for His kingdom.

The Magician archetype is the most difficult one for me. There have been so many times in my life when God has closed a door that I truly thought I was meant to pass through only to open a window and give me a new plan. Sometimes these changes seem very small but end up changing my direction entirely. Sometimes they are huge and for awhile I cannot find the window.

Often, I don't have a sense of where I'm going, only that I'm on the move and the journey of my life continues. Several years ago, my husband and I were living in a town that we had called home for twenty-five years. We were comfortable there. My husband had his place in community, I had mine, and we had our place together. I loved what God had given me to do. I was working with children and families, and I was leading a team of volunteers. It was my dream! Neither of my children lived nearby, and since my experience with cancer, I did not work full time, yet I was satisfied and happy with my life, my work.

Everything changed in a heartbeat—a telephone call actually! I no longer was able to do my work, work that I believed God had given me to do. What would I do with my time? Why had God closed that door? Wasn't I good enough? I knew scripture said that Jesus came to divide families, but could that mean friends and organizations as well? Why had some people I dearly loved turned their back on me?

It was a devasting time when nothing seemed to make sense and I was in a panic. At times it hurt to breathe, and it seemed everything I thought I could count on had changed. I felt betrayed! I was not the only scapegoat in this situation, but I knew I was set to take a fall, and not for the first time. People I thought I could depend on were not available to me and didn't support me. Other people never left my side and encouraged me every day during this period of transition. I was living through the Orphan and sometimes toxic Orphan archetype. I felt isolated and alone. My life seemed to stall, and the transition seemed to span forever. Special celebrations came and went, but people I had thought would always be in my life were not there. Life had changed, and it was uncomfortable! I found myself fighting to put things back the way they had been.

This is when I transitioned to the Warrior archetype, at times the toxic Warrior. However, no matter how hard I tried, there was no way back. When I was able to think things through, I knew our path was in a different direction. Turning to God, we asked him to show us the direction He had planned for us. He is the one constant. He will never leave us or forsake us (Deuteronomy 31:6).

Our place in community had changed so significantly that we began to think a complete overhaul of our lives was required, and my husband and I entered the Wanderer archetype. Our house was too big for us now that our children were grown and living on their own. We had always planned to downsize at some point, so we decided through prayer that a move would be a healthy and beneficial choice. We put our house on the market, never thinking that it would sell quickly, but it did. Within a week, the deal closed, and we had two months to find a new home in a new town!

Our daughter and her husband had recently moved to a small town on Vancouver Island. Coincidentally, in our retirement, we had planned to move to a nearby vacation beach resort town. As a result of prayer and with conviction that this course of action was God's will for us, we began to look for a new home somewhere in the area. We were looking in several little towns, but nothing seemed quite right.

My husband, though able to retire and almost of retirement age, didn't feel ready at this time, so he was looking for a position up island. Much to our surprise, though we continued to pray asking for direction and guidance, a position was posted with the company my husband was currently working for in the same town where our daughter lived. He applied for the position but wondered if he would be hired, considering he was nearing retirement age and moving to a new location. Within a day of his interview, we got the call. He had a new job in a new town! It was an answer to our prayer and a nudge in a clear direction, but now the search for a house became earnest.

We had a starting date for my husband's new job and the buyers for our house had a possession date; both worked out to be around the same day. However, we did not have a lead on a suitable house. We arranged to see a realtor on a weekend and searched everywhere. Finally, there it was, the house. Not just any house. This was a little rancher that fulfilled almost everything on our wish list!

We submitted an offer. It was an intense buying process and there were give and take moments in the deal, but we knew in our hearts that God was in control of every coincidence. In the intense final moments of the sale, we sealed the deal and negotiated a completion date on the same date as the house we were selling. We moved on a Friday and my husband started his new job on the next Monday! We could not have planned this move or change of work any better, but it was not our plan. We believe it was God's plan and His will for us. He had changed life's lemons to lemonade! The Magician, I believe the Holy Spirit, was at work in us with supernatural knowledge and understanding—and timing.

The story does not end here! Our son, with his wife and kids, was living and working in another province. However, due to employment cuts, he lost his job. He quickly found another position in another town in the same province but lost that position due to a sluggish economy. At the end of his rope, and totally unexpectedly, he found a position in this same town where we are living. Our whole family is in one place now! Could I have planned it? I certainly could dream about it, and it is the desire of my heart to have our family together, but only God could accomplish the plan! "Take delight in the Lord, and he will give you the desires of your heart" (Psalm 37:4). I think this was the Holy Spirit and the Magician archetype at work changing our circumstances and leading us into a better future as we relied on and surrendered to the God of the universe and His transformative power. It is as scripture says:

> Jesus looked at them and said, "With man this is impossible, but with God all things are possible" (Matthew 19:26)

SHARON'S CONCLUSION

THE MESSAGE BIBLE says, "Test yourself, make sure you are solid in the faith . . . Give yourself regular check ups" (*Message Bible,* 2018, Corinthians 13:5–9). This verse speaks to my belief that we begin with self-examination in order to know where we are and our motivation and to explore the state of our relationship with God. How am I acting? How am I treating others? Where does that thought come from? What do I believe? The answer to these questions are found in the following verses.

"Do unto others as you would have them do unto you" (Matthew 7:12) and "Treat your neighbour as yourself" (Luke 10:27) are the two great commandments from the Lord. I complain and hurt deeply at some of the ways I have been treated, and then when I apply Matthew 7:12, to my own behaviour, I begin to understand that I am being treated the same way I have treated others and that I am treating others as I was treated. To peel the onion skin even deeper, I treat others the way I treat myself which is the way I was treated growing up in my family and by peers as a teen. I was not treated well, did not learn how to treat myself well, and became my parents to myself and others.

Only through this deep, honest, vulnerable exploration of self can I begin to understand myself. Only in the admission that I want to change can I begin the process of change; this is the first step on a journey that ultimately leads to understanding I cannot do this in my own strength. I need help. The belief that God is my strength is a basic foundation of my life.

When I walk for a time with someone on their journey, I come to a point in the relationship when I ask these following questions:

Where do you get your authority?

Is the behaviour that is "right" today also "right" tomorrow?

Do your beliefs change as social mores change?

What is your standard to measure your actions/thoughts?

What informs you when you stray from your beliefs?

When I apply those questions to myself, I answer that my truth comes from scripture that is the Word of truth.

When I was walking in the truth of my own eyes, I still knew when I was straying from the truth of scripture. That still-small voice was omnipresent. My journey out of conflict either brought me to the place of surrender or had me let go completely of all truth and be like a weathervane. There was a dark place inside me that knew there was no way out if I did that. All hope would be gone in this place, and I would be losing a part of my mind. I choose to surrender to God and His mercy and grace.

I am aware of myself and others using the phrase, "Well, I don't care about . . ." I now catch myself and say, "I care about . . . and I care more about what God says/wants." This applies to our beliefs and values. I care about what you think of me, and I care more about being honest and what I think of myself.

The learning in these archetypes and in the theory of abandonment is a pathway, a vehicle to explore yourself and come to an understanding of self and then choose where/how you want to live. The abandonment theory is the one I use the most for my own healing as well as in my practice with clients.

I sincerely hope we have demonstrated that scripture and psychology are not mutually exclusive. Christianity concepts can be found in many psychological theories. We in no way are saying Christianity informs nor underpins all psychological theories. We are also not offering the opinion that these are the only archetypes. These are the ones Carol Pearson uses in her book, *The Hero Within*.

Our prayer throughout the writing of this book was that if it would speak to even one person and help in their healing process, then all was well.

Perhaps this book, the idea, the co-writing was all for our healing. If so, I am very grateful.

Kathy's Conclusion

"Jesus Christ is the same yesterday and today and forever."
—Hebrews 13:8

THIS WRITING HAS been an adventure and a learning curve, a journey towards self-understanding and to a clearer understanding of my faith. Like everyone else, I have struggled with life's lemons. At times, I wondered how I found myself in certain situations or in intense struggle and emotional pain. Sometimes, I know I make bad decisions and I then struggle with the consequences, but sometimes bad things just seem to happen. My mom would often tell me to look up to Jesus. When reminded, at times, I would step back onto the journey of faith, but other times, I've side-stepped and wandered away from my faith, losing track of the constant unfailing love and person of Christ. As I fell farther and farther away from Jesus, I felt helpless and totally out of control of my circumstances. This is when I turned to counselling (psychology) to help me better understand myself, my journey, God's Word, and His will for me.

I learned during the journey that prayer, studying the Bible, and psychology can help me understand the human condition and how my mind works. God gave me intelligence and free will. I can exercise them both. My choice is to either surrender my life and will to God or to lean on my own strength and understanding. For me, the latter way doesn't work well! When I lose sight of God and of His plan for my life and the knowledge that I can do nothing on my own, my life seems to spiral out of control. When I realize that all things are possible with God and give Him control of my life, my path comes into focus again.

Through the years, I learned that it is a constant battle to turn my life and my will to the Saviour, to trust Him to "make my path straight" and not to rely on my own intelligence, or lack thereof, and my own plans. When I leave my life with Him, He will give me the strength and understanding to persevere and journey onward, opening and closing doors as I go. Psychology, particularly working with archetypes and the abandonment theory, helps me find the steps towards healing and returning to God. Looking back at the path, I see God carrying me through my entire life.

When I wrote about people living thousands of years ago, their stories found in the Bible, these people became more real to me. Their stories tell us that they experienced life in much the same way as we do today even though our culture has changed dramatically in thousands of years and our life circumstances look totally different. The archetypes appeared and worked through their lives just as they work through our lives. The stories I selected to tell are favourites of mine and I think demonstrate the characteristics of the archetypes well, but there are countless other stories in the Bible that demonstrate the timeless workings of human psychology. As King Soloman said in Ecclesiastes 1:9, "What has been will be again, what has been done will be done again; there is nothing new under the sun."

In conclusion, I leave the book with God and you, the reader. I think we all wrestle with abandonment issues and, no matter what we call them, we all wrestle with and circulate through the archetypes: the fall of the Innocent to the Orphan, the love of the Altruist, the curiosity of the Wanderer, the determination of the Warrior, the intuitive power of the Magician, and many others that are not explored in this discussion. If you ask God into your heart to journey with you, He doesn't promise a life free of struggle and challenges, but He does promise He will never leave you or forsake you. He will always walk beside you and share your burdens.

May God bless you and hold you close, filling your heart with love, joy, and peace.

All quotes from the Bible are from the New International Version (NIV) (1995) unless otherwise stated.

Scripture quotations marked The Message are taken from The Message (2003) Remixed by Eugene H. Peterson, Nav Press.

"All scripture is given by inspiration of God, and is profitable for doctrine, for reproof, for correction, for instruction in righteousness." (2 Timothy 3:16)

REFERENCES

Anderson, S. (2000). *The journey from abandonment to healing*. Berkley Publishing Company.

Dickens, C. (1843). *A Christmas carol in prose being a ghost story of Christmas*. Chapman & Hall.

Dictionary.com (n.d.). Archetype. In *Dictionary.com* online dictionary. Retrieved April 12, 2024, from https://www.dictionary.com/browse/archetype

Dictionary.com (n.d.). Sacrifice. In *Dictionary.com* online dictionary. Retrieved April 12, 2024, from https://www.dictionary.com/browse/sacrifice.

Hillman, J. (1975). *Revisioning psychology*. Harper & Row.

Jeffers, S. (1987). *Face the fear and do it anyway*. New York, Fawcett Columbine.

Maslow, A.H. (1966). The psychology of science: A reconnaissance. Harper & Row.

Moore, T. (2017). *Ageless soul: The lifelong journey toward meaning and joy*. St. Martin's Press.

Peck, M. S. (1978). *The road less travelled; A new psychology of love, traditional values and spiritual growth*. Simon & Schuster.

Peason, C. (1986). *The hero within: Six archetypes we live by.* Harper & Row.

Seigal. B. (1986). *Love, medicine and miracles.* Harper & Row

Van der Kolk, B. (2015). *The body keeps the score; Brain, mind, and body in the healing of trauma.* Penguin Books.

Wortitz, J. (1986). *Struggle for intimacy.* Health Communications Inc.

About the Authors
Sharon Priest

I HAVE ALWAYS BELIEVED many psychological theories are rooted in Scripture. It is my experience that therapists are not well spoken of from the pulpit.

In my thirty plus years as a mental health counsellor (Master of Social Work and Registered Clinical Counsellor) and my thirty years or so as a Christian I witnessed many people struggle and benefit from psychology. When wounds are healed, we become more the person we were created to be.

I honour the courageous people who are on their journey and feel privileged to accompany them.

My many years working with First Nation people fills my soul; it is like I have come home to myself.

I am mother of three adult children, five biological grandchildren and one chosen grandchild. God has blessed me beyond riches, and I marvel at His work as they journey.

In God all things are possible; even lessening the gap.

About the Authors

Kathryn Colegrave

TODAY, I LIVE with my husband, and I am blessed with two married adult children and three amazing grandchildren. When my children were young and I was in my thirties, I was diagnosed with cancer. During the radical treatment that followed, I trusted Jesus and the Bible. However, I was struggling to understand what was happening. Confused, I turned to psychology even though I thought I might have to choose between the church or counselling.

After my illness, I built a career in children's ministry. As Sunday School Director, I took a leadership role by developing programs, connecting with families, and building adult teaching teams. Later I attended University and Seminary, learning more about Jesus and Bible teachings. The relationship between the stories in the Bible, the Abandonment Theory and the Archetypes creates a sort of bridge for me, lessening the gap between scripture and psychology.